REFLECTIONS

Reflections

HERMANN HESSE

SELECTED FROM HIS BOOKS AND LETTERS
BY VOLKER MICHELS

TRANSLATED BY RALPH MANHEIM

Farrar, Straus and Giroux

NEW YORK

Acknowledgment is made to publishers of earlier translations of works by Hermann Hesse, as follows: excerpts from *Demian*, copyright 1925 by S. Fischer Verlag, by permission of Harper and Row, Publishers, Inc.; excerpts from *Steppenwolf*, copyright 1927 by S. Fischer Verlag AG, Berlin, copyright 1955 by Hermann Hesse, Montagnola, by permission of Holt, Rinehart and Winston, Inc.; excerpts from *The Glass Bead Game*, copyright 1943 by Fretz & Wasmuth Verlag, Berlin, by permission of Holt, Rinehart and Winston, Inc.; excerpts from *Siddhartha*, copyright 1950 by Hermann Hesse, Montagnola, by permission of New Directions Publishing Corporation, earlier translation by Hilda Rosner, copyright 1951 by New Directions Publishing Corporation; excerpts from the following books by permission of Peter Owen, Ltd., London: *Gertrude,* copyright 1955 by Suhrkamp Verlag, Berlin; *Beneath the Wheel*, copyright 1953 by Hermann Hesse, Montagnola; *Narcissus and Goldmund*, copyright 1930, 1957 by Hermann Hesse, Montagnola; *Peter Camenzind*, copyright 1953 by Hermann Hesse, Montagnola; *The Journey to the East*, © 1956 by Hermann Hesse; *Siddhartha*, copyright 1950 by Hermann Hesse, Montagnola; *Demian*, copyright 1925 by S. Fischer Verlag

Translation copyright © 1974 by Farrar, Straus and Giroux, Inc.

Translated from the German, *Lektüre für Minuten,*
copyright © 1971 Suhrkamp Verlag, Frankfurt am Main

Library of Congress Cataloging in Publication Data
Hesse, Hermann, 1877–1962.
   Reflections.
   Translation of Lektüre für Minuten.
   I.   Title.
PT2617.E85A6   1974b   838'.9'1209   73–87700

Aphorisms are something like jewels;
rarity increases their value,
and they are enjoyable only in small doses.

HERMANN HESSE

Contents

POLITICS

Politics

Every politician in the world is all for revolution, reason, and disarmament—but only in enemy countries, not in his own.

[1]

Why is it that only those who hope to profit by it come out for the self-determination of nations?

[2]

No one was thinking of war; they were all arming just in case, because rich people like to see iron walls around their money.

[3]

All history seems to revolve around aims and opinions or ways of changing the world, which soon prove not to have been taken very seriously. Only yesterday people were fired by lofty ideals; today it is quite otherwise. That's what is so depressing.

[4]

The value of a future order will be exactly as great as the sacrifices we make *today*.

[5]

The greatest threat to our world and its peace comes from those who want war, who prepare for it, and who, by

3

holding out vague promises of a future peace or by instilling fear of foreign aggression, try to make us accomplices to their plans.

[6]

War does not advance the world, it merely postpones, merely provides men's passions with ephemeral new goals. Afterwards, sooner or later, our social misery will be with us again, as appalling as ever.

[7]

Patriotism subordinates the individual to something bigger. But it is not really prized as a virtue until the shooting starts.

[8]

I like to think of myself as a patriot, but even more so as a man. Where the two disagree, I say the man is right.

[9]

Just as every dead soldier marks the eternal repetition of an error, so truth must eternally be repeated in a thousand forms.

[10]

No one is guilty. The world is bombed and burned and devastated and those who do it are perfectly innocent. They are "exponents" or "factors" or something equally clever, not men, not moral, responsible beings under God. I wouldn't give a red cent for such talk.

[11]

As I see it, the love of heroism is permissible only in those who risk their own lives; in others, it is not only a delu-

4

sion but also, I believe, a ruthlessness, which fills me with shame and anger.

[12]

Anyone who shirks the labors, sacrifices, and dangers that his people must undergo is a coward. But no less a coward and traitor is the man who betrays the principles of thought to material interests, who, for example, is willing to let the holders of power decide how much is two times two. To sacrifice intellectual integrity, love of truth, the laws and methods of thought to any other interest, even that of the fatherland, is treason. When in the battle of interests and slogans the truth, like the individual, is in danger of being devalued, disfigured, and trampled under foot, our one duty is to resist and to save the truth—or rather, the striving for truth—for that is our highest article of faith.

[13]

It is better to suffer injustice than to commit it. Any attempt to gain desired ends by illicit means is wrong. Generals regard such ideas as foolishness and statesmen laugh at them, but they are old and tested truths.

[14]

A war doesn't fall out of the clear sky. Like every other human undertaking, it requires preparation; to make it a possibility and then a reality, the care and cooperation of many are needed. It is desired, prepared for, and proposed by those men and powers who stand to gain by it. Either it brings them direct cash profit, as in the case of the armaments industry (and as soon as war breaks out, how many previously harmless industries become war industries, and how automatically money flows their way!), or it brings them advantage in the form of prestige, respect, and power, as in the case of unemployed generals and colonels.

[15]

The cancer that is devouring our whole world is the hypertrophic state, which has become an idol and end in itself, with its bureaucrats whose automatic striving it is to devise more and more useless offices and formalities, so as to make themselves indispensable and increase their number.

[16]

In my opinion we owe the present state of mankind to two mental disorders: the megalomania of technology and the megalomania of nationalism. It is they that have given the present-day world its face and its view of itself; they have given us two world wars and their aftermaths and before their frenzy is spent they will have other, similar consequences.

Resistance to these two world diseases is today the most important task and justification of the human spirit. In this resistance my own life has played a part, a ripple in the stream.

[17]

I believe that our life, the average life of the present-day Occidental, is so loathsome that it can be borne only by clods, idiots, people without nerves, taste, or sensibility. "Heroism" has become the ideal of our age—a heroism that ends in the trenches at forty below zero. If people are able to endure this life, it is only because they have already lost the habit of exercising man's best and finest gifts.

[18]

One is amazed time and again by the amount of intelligence, method, and organization that go into the doing of senseless things, and no less by the amount of unreason and naïveté with which peoples make virtue of necessity and fashion ideologies out of carnage. Man is just that stupid and naïve.

[19]

The more individuals capable of watching the world theater calmly and critically, the less danger of monumental mass stupidities—first of all, wars.

[20]

Today political reason is no longer at the seat of political power. If catastrophes are to be avoided or attenuated, an influx of intelligence and intuition from unofficial circles is indispensable.

[21]

God bless the simple souls who were able to love themselves and hate their enemies, the patriots who were never driven to self-doubt, because they themselves were never in the least to blame for the misery and ruin of their country, but always the French or the Russians or the Jews, no matter, as long as it was somebody else, an "enemy"! Maybe these people, nine-tenths of humanity, were really happy in their barbaric primitive religion; maybe they were enviably lighthearted in their armor of stupidity or of calculated hostility to thought.

[22]

The heroism that looks so good in orders of the day and victory communiqués is sentimentality. When a poor defeated soldier takes his own life at the foot of his flag, or when a man who has had bad luck turns his back on friendship, love, and kindness because he thinks they have let him down, such behavior impresses no one outside the theater. To gnash the teeth is not heroism, and to pocket clenched fists while waiting for some distant revenge is pathetic.

[23]

The Germans are extremely sentimental, and when, as so often, their sentimentality enters into combination with brutality, it is intolerable.

[24]

It is well known that the most blatant atavisms feel the strongest need to disguise themselves as modern and progressive.

[25]

I regard a relapse into Fascist mass hypnosis, if only for a brief period, as possible in several countries, and not only those of Europe. The more the individual and the family lose their standing and influence in the advanced countries, the more they are replaced by collective regimentation, the greater will be the danger.

[26]

The Fascist experiment is regressive, useless, stupid, and degrading. The Communist experiment, on the other hand, is one which mankind had to make and which, even if it has bogged down in dreary inhumanity, will have to be made time and time again, not for the sake of any stupid "dictatorship of the proletariat," but in order to bring about some sort of justice and brotherhood between the bourgeoisie and the proletariat. In view of the similar methods employed by Fascism and Communism, this is easily forgotten.

[27]

In order to rule, it is by no means necessary, as some conceited intellectuals suppose, to be stupid and brutal.

8

What is needed to rule is an unflagging pleasure in outward activity, a passion for identifying oneself with aims and purposes, and also a certain quickness and unscrupulousness in the choice of means. All these are qualities that a scholar should not and does not have, since for him contemplation is more important than action. He has learned to be as scrupulous and distrustful as possible in his choice of means.

[28]

Primitive man hates what he fears, and in certain strata of his soul, civilized, educated man is a primitive. Thus the hatred of peoples and races for other peoples and races is based not on superiority and strength, but on insecurity and weakness.

A truly superior man, a real master, will pity the man he knows himself superior to, and perhaps occasionally despise him, but never hate him.

[29]

Sometimes all history strikes me as a picture book reflecting man's blindest and most violent craving: the craving for forgetfulness. Doesn't every generation—by censorship, silence, and ridicule—expunge the memory of the very things that seemed most important to the preceding generation? Didn't whole peoples succeed in forgetting a long and monstrously cruel war for years, in denying, repressing, and spiriting away its memory? And now that these same peoples have rested awhile, aren't they trying, with the help of exciting war movies, to remember what they themselves did and suffered a few years ago?

[30]

People keep looking for "freedom" and "happiness" somewhere in the past, for fear of being reminded that they themselves are responsible for what they make of their lives. For a few years they drink and make merry, then they settle down and become serious gentlemen in the government service.

[31]

Every human being is a unique individual. Any attempt to replace the personal conscience by a collective conscience does violence to the individual and is the first step toward totalitarianism.

[32]

I have often seen a room full of people, a city full of people, a country full of people seized with an intoxication and frenzy in which many individuals become a unit, a homogeneous mass, and all individuality is extinguished. In a surge of unanimity, all individual impulses merge into a single mass impulse and hundreds, thousands, or millions are seized with a rapture, a selfless devotion and heroism, which express themselves at first in outcries, tears, and touching declarations of brotherhood and end in war, madness, and rivers of blood. My instinct as an individualist and artist has always warned me most urgently against this capacity of men for becoming drunk on collective suffering, collective pride, collective hatred, and collective honor. When this morbid exaltation becomes perceptible in a room, a hall, a village, a city, or a country, I grow cold and distrustful; a shudder comes over me, for already, while most of my fellow men are still weeping with rapture and enthusiasm, still cheering and venting protestations of brotherhood, I see blood flowing and cities going up in flames.

[33]

I do not believe that man will be "better" in the future; I do not believe that man is ever better or worse; he is always the same. But at certain times the demonic erupts into mankind not only secretly, among criminals and psychopaths, but openly and on a large scale; it takes on a political life and sweeps whole nations off their feet.

[34]

Today I observe with amazement, for I have given up any real attempt to understand it, how the most childish, the most bestial political drives set themselves up as "philosophies," etc., and even adopt the gestures of religion. Though Marxist socialism is infinitely more intelligent, these systems have one thing in common with it, namely, their belief that man can be turned into an almost exclusively political animal, which is not true. I believe that the convulsions of the present-day world are largely the consequences of this fallacy.

[35]

I have not withdrawn from the problems of the day in the course of my development and I have never, as my political critics claim, lived in an ivory tower. But the first and most urgent of my problems has never been the state, society, or the church; it is the individual man, the personality, the unique, unstandardized individual.

[36]

When a man demands a good deal of himself, I understand and approve; but when he extends this demand to others and makes his life a "struggle" for the good, I can only withhold judgment, because I attribute no value at all to struggle, action, or opposition. I believe that every attempt to change the world leads to war and violence. I am unable to join any opposition movement, because I do not approve of the ultimate consequences and because I regard the injustice and wickedness of this world as incurable.

What we can and should change is ourselves: our impatience, our egoism (including intellectual egoism), our sense of injury, our lack of love and forbearance. I regard every other attempt to change the world, even if it springs from the best intentions, as futile.

[37]

Our contacts with the cruelty and envy, the malice and often unfathomable hatred of our fellow men are always terrifying, though we should know what to expect, though we should know that most people are only half human and that there are many beasts among them. We are as much beset and threatened by baseness as we are by death. Our horror at it is probably related to the fact that though we do not respond to baseness with baseness, we secretly know or suspect that the conditions under which most people live are unworthy and must necessarily engender baseness, and that we, who have been somewhat better brought up, who are somewhat better educated and more spoiled, bear our secret share in the horror of prevailing conditions.

[38]

Not only do I regard Communism as justified; I also regard its coming as self-evident—it would win out even if we were all against it. Those who side with Communism today say yes to the future. And now, no doubt, you will ask why, if I believe in the soundness of Communism and feel for the oppressed, I do not join you in the struggle and put my pen at the disposal of the Party. That is a hard question to answer, for it involves things that for me are sacred and binding but for you hardly exist. Though the prospect of brothers and comrades, of fellowship with a world of like-minded men, attracts me very considerably,

I resolutely refuse to join the Party or enlist my writing in the service of a program.

[39]

I believe in Communism as a program for the coming period of mankind; I regard it as indispensable and inevitable. But I do not for that reason believe that Communism has better answers to the great problems of life than any earlier wisdom. I believe that, after a hundred years of theory and the great Russian experiment, it has not only the right, but the duty as well, to extend itself to the world, and I sincerely hope and trust that it will succeed in doing away with hunger, so relieving mankind of a great nightmare. I do not believe that this will accomplish what the religions, laws, and philosophies of earlier centuries could not achieve. I do not believe that, beyond the proclamation of every man's right to bread and human dignity, Communism is truer or better than any earlier form of belief. It has its roots in the nineteenth century, in the arid, arrogant intellectualism of an overbearing, loveless, unimaginative professordom.

[40]

I advise no one not to join a party, but I do tell everyone that if he does so at too early an age, he is running the risk of bartering his own judgment for the pleasure of being surrounded by comrades. Moreover, I point out to everyone, including my own sons, that support of a program and membership in a party must not be a game, but must call for an attitude of responsibility; in other words, that anyone who commits himself to revolution must not only put his own life in the service of the cause, but must also be able and willing to kill, be it with machine guns or gas.

[41]

Fascism and Bolshevism are two enemy brothers, but brothers all the same. Where the one grows, it fertilizes the field for the other and calls it into being.

[42]

I have never likened the undertakings of Hitler, Mussolini, or Franco, which are regressive, stupid, and useless, to the great undertaking of Communism, which is absolutely necessary. And yet the men into whose hands the power structure of Communism has fallen have been guilty of every kind of terror and brutality, every form of violence to man. There really seems to be only one hope for man: not to change the world and others, but in some degree to change and improve himself. The salvation of the world rests secretly upon those who manage to do so.

[43]

I have no taste for politics; otherwise I would have become a revolutionary long ago.

[44]

Apart from Marx's much larger dimensions, the main difference between Marx and me is this: Marx wanted to change the world, I want to change the individual man. He spoke to the masses, I to individuals.

[45]

The future probably belongs to Communism. But then the question arises: How long will this future last? In 1500, the future undoubtedly belonged to Protestantism.

[46]

No one with a sense of intellectual responsibility can become a Communist without asking himself the question: "Do I want and approve of revolution? Can I support the killing of people in order that other people's lot may perhaps be improved?" That is the problem. I do not grant myself the right to revolution and murder. This does not prevent me from regarding the masses as innocent even when somewhere on earth their misery makes them explode with rage and kill. But if I myself were to join in I should not be innocent, because I should be going against one of my few absolutely sacred principles.

[47]

Revolution is nothing other than war; like war, it is a "continuation of politics by other methods."

[48]

As long as Communism sets itself the aim, not of distributing power and property among all, but of establishing the "dictatorship of the proletariat," it is a regression from Marx, and as long as its beneficiaries are not the people but a small clique of party bosses, it is not worth bothering with.

[49]

Obviously, the Communism that Marx had in mind eighty years ago in the *Manifesto* has nothing in common with the fury that is raging today under that name. The worst of it for those of us who think is that the intervening degeneration of Communism has very much diminished the prospects of a viable, human form of authentic Communism, and has enormously strengthened and seemingly justified all those trends that hark back to ideas that were current long before Marx.

[50]

Most people are devoid of personal convictions; they have only those of their caste; ninety-nine percent of both capitalists and socialists support opinions that their minds are quite incapable of testing.

[51]

Regimentation, however well intended, is contrary to nature. It leads to fanaticism and war.

[52]

Today the cult of social and collective responsibility is such that it is often the egoists and the morally sick who take desperate flight into ideologies and parties and distrust the rest of us, who take social considerations—that is, civic duty and the ideal of brotherly love—for granted.

[53]

So far in my life, which has been rich in acquaintance with people of many countries, I have met amazingly few whose political opinions deviated significantly from those expressed in the editorials they read. Consequently, I find myself unable to regard political opinion as an authentic mark of personality and take far more interest in what stands behind a man's opinions, in the man himself.

[54]

You are right in saying that we are defenseless against the state and similar powers. But in my opinion you are dead wrong in inferring that our only way out is to defend ourselves "unscrupulously." The very thing we must not do is complain that the world is unscrupulous and be just as unscrupulous ourselves. Our privilege and distinction are precisely that we do have scruples, that we do not regard everything as permissible, that we do not participate in hatred and killing and every other kind of bestiality.

The uncouth gesture of "shitting on the whole business" was not invented by you. It has been seen hundreds of times in history. We can tolerate it, we can understand it as the reaction of weak, uncultivated people to cruel abuse of power—but we cannot approve of it and call it right.

[55]

Whether the workers kill the factory owners, or Russians and Germans shoot at each other, nothing is accomplished but a change of ownership.

[56]

Person and program are not the same. It is possible to derive more satisfaction and to learn more from opponents, even declared enemies, than from those who share our convictions only with their reason, only in words.

[57]

"Personality" is no longer universally regarded as an ideal, as it was in Goethe's day. Today, both in the proletarian and in the bourgeois camp, the individual personality is rejected as an end in itself—the common aim is to breed not outstanding individuals but a normal, healthy, efficient average man. Under these circumstances industry thrives. But in Germany, for instance, this last brief period has shown that vital functions of the body politic languish and incur fatal crises for lack of the energy, responsibility, and inner purity that only high-minded individuals can supply. The hideous degeneration of political life, of the parties, of parliamentarianism points clearly to the absence of such individuals, and meanwhile the very same parties that make life in their midst impossible for anyone who is even slightly above average clamor for a "strong man."

[58]

To my mind there are two histories of mankind, the one political, the other spiritual. In neither is anything resembling progress discernible. Whether Samson smites the Philistines with a bone or Hitler fires rockets at England, it's the same thing. Nor has there been any perceptible progress in philosophy from the Upanishads to Heidegger. On the other hand, the two histories are very different. So-called political history, whatever segment of it we choose to examine, is ugly, cruel, diabolical. Whereas the history of languages, of ideas, of the arts is in every period replete with beautiful images and admirable flowers.

[59]

In spite of everything, my love has never gone out to the revolutionary aspect of the French Revolution of 1789, but always to the aristocrats who died with dignity. For despite the Christian, democratic, and socialist truths, which retain their validity in the flatter realms of life, all culture and beauty are rooted in nobility, in an inborn superiority of the senses, mind, and soul. Today it is the nobler who are doomed to die, because they have wakeful and sensitive eyes, ears, and souls.

[60]

It is not only armed international war whose horror and absurdity have become clear to me. It is all war, every kind of violence, of aggressive self-seeking, all disregard for life and abuse of one's fellow man. By peace I mean not only military and political peace, but also every man's peace with himself and his neighbors, the harmony of a life full of meaning and love.

[61]

Humanity and politics are essentially incompatible. Both are necessary, but to serve both at once is hardly possible.

Politics demands partisanship, humanity forbids partisanship.

[62]

People laugh at those who refuse military service. In my opinion, they are the most precious manifestation of our times, even though some of them give odd reasons for their attitudes. Already a considerable advance has been made: serious consideration is being given to a bill providing that conscientious objectors be given an opportunity to do work of a nonmilitary nature during their term of service. It may not pass—not yet, that is—but it undoubtedly will one of these days. And perhaps a time will come when for every three soldiers there will be ten men doing civilian service, when the military trade, insofar as it still exists, will be reserved for the born ruffians and blackguards. But all this would never have come about if a few men spurred by strong feeling had not had the courage to defy public opinion and refuse to serve.

[63]

From the earliest human history known to us, there has always been war, and there will always be war as long as the majority of men are unable to share in the life of the spirit. There will be war for a long time to come, probably forever. And yet the elimination of war remains our noblest goal. The researcher who is looking for a means of preventing disease will not throw his work away because an epidemic has broken out. Much less will "peace on earth" and friendship among men of good will ever cease to be our ideal. Human culture arises through the sublimation of animal drives, through shame, imagination, and knowledge. The belief that life is worth living is the ultimate content and solace of every art, even though all those who have praised life have been doomed to die. This wretched world war must convince us more profoundly than ever before that love is better than hate, understanding than anger, peace than war.

[64]

During the war we often heard it said that because of its sheer magnitude and the enormity of the mechanism it released, this war would so frighten future generations that they would never again make war. This is absolutely false. Fear is without educational value. No war can discourage those who enjoy killing. Rational considerations play the most infinitesimal part in human actions. A man can be fully convinced of the absurdity of an action and nevertheless throw himself into it with fervor.

[65]

What interests me in a man's attitude is this: is he "political"; that is, does he believe in the methods of politics, the ultimate and most powerful of which are always cannon? Or, disbelieving in politics, does he tend instead to orient his life and thinking toward God, toward a timeless and transcendent mid-point, not in the sense of a reasoned philosophy, but in the sense of service and sacrifice? For you my standpoint is not subject to discussion; nor is it for me, since it is not a matter of choice, but my destiny. Whether I am "right," it is not for me to decide. As I see it, no one is right; the struggles between conflicting opinions and programs are not rational, hence essentially avoidable, but tragic and unavoidable. To my mind, it matters not at all whether Hitler or Trotsky or someone else commands the cannon—heaven help him if he sincerely believes in the value of what he is doing; he will not change or improve the world, for he is not at its pivotal point, which for men of my faith is situated within each soul. I hold that it is permissible for each one of us to die for his faith, but not to kill for his faith.

[66]

There is nothing more detestable than borders, nothing stupider than borders. They are like cannon, like generals: as long as reason, humanity, and peace prevail, we take no notice of them, we smile at them—but once war and madness break out, they become important and sacred.

[67]

The soldier who shoots down the enemy is almost always regarded as a greater patriot than the peasant who tills his land to the best of his ability. Because the peasant derives advantage from what he does. Oddly enough, a virtue that brings its possessor pleasure and profit is held suspect in our intricate ethical system. Why should this be so? Because we are accustomed to gain advantage only at the expense of others. Because we are full of distrust and imagine that we must always desire what belongs to someone else.

[68]

When a naughty child resists punishment and correction on the ground that other children are just as naughty, we smile and have our answer ready. But just like this naughty child, we have been protesting throughout this dreary war that our enemies are at least as bad as we are.

[69]

My attitude toward all officialdom and government authority is unchanged: they make me gnash my teeth. I find it preposterous and deplorable that entire peoples are still convulsively bowing, scraping, and carrying out orders when the governments themselves don't know what they want or what they ought to do.

[70]

An accusation is never nullified by the fact that it cannot be proved in court.

[71]

Sincere and more or less intelligent people are not so frequent; when such people come into conflict with each other, they ought, if possible, to strengthen and purify each other in the process.

[72]

I am a stove, but might just as well be a statesman. I have a big mouth, give little warmth, spew smoke through a pipe, bear a good name, and arouse great memories.

[73]

Thus far, unfortunately, our experience with quotations from the Bible in the mouths of statesmen has not been happy.

[74]

Have the politicians ever been right? Isn't a line of Hölderlin's poetry worth more than all the wisdom of potentates?

[75]

An intelligent man strives for power, if only in order to do "good." Herein lies his greatest danger, in the striving for power, in its misuse, in his desire to command, in terror. Trotsky, who couldn't bear to see a peasant beaten, has had no scruples about slaughtering hundreds of thousands for the sake of his ideas.

[76]

In choosing and arranging his little words in the midst of a world that may be destroyed tomorrow, a poet does exactly the same as the anemones and cowslips and other flowers that are now growing in every meadow. In the midst of a world that may be blanketed in poison gas tomorrow, they carefully form their corollas and calyxes, with five or four or seven petals, smooth or indented, all with the greatest precision and as prettily as can be.

[77]

Violence is evil and for those who have come awake nonviolence is the only way. It will never be the way of all and never of those in power, of those who make history and wage wars. The earth will never be a paradise, and mankind will never be one and reconciled with God. But if we know which side we are on, we live more freely and serenely. We must always be prepared to suffer violence, but never be ready to kill.

[78]

Only in war is killing permitted, because in war no one kills out of hatred or envy or for his own profit; everyone merely does what the collectivity demands.

[79]

The ants also wage wars, the bees also have states, the hamsters also amass riches.

[80]

In my opinion, a government official who "wants nothing to do with politics" is a parasite, and a soldier who lays waste the countryside and shoots at people day after day, with nothing on his mind but heroism and military honor and never a thought of the blood that is being shed and the cities that are being devastated, is a simpleton. That's the way most officials and soldiers are and think; there is little to choose between them.

[81]

23

Anyone who works for spiritual values will always have the hurrah-patriots and the pocketbook-patriots against him, often combined in the same persons.

[82]

It is possible to regard patriotism as atavistic and yet belong to bowling clubs and poetry societies.

[83]

For me, "fatherland" and patriotic ideals have ceased to exist; they are mere window dressing for the gentlemen who are making preparations for the next slaughter.

[84]

Formerly, when young men drunk on tragedy and grandeur were going about with knapsacks and guitars, they were charming in a comical kind of way; but they have quickly adapted themselves to warfare, conquest, and torture.

[85]

When people talk of our times in years to come, I believe they will discern a tendency toward religious overestimation of the collectivity and a marked "flight" from personal to social preoccupations. I am unable to share this view that the concerns of the community are intrinsically higher and more sacred than those of the individual. Social duties are indeed important, but they are not the only duties and not the highest, for there is no such thing as a "supreme" duty. The pious, God-oriented man of earlier cultures performed his social duties as a matter of course, though his sole concern was his personal relationship with God. And so it has always been, among the ancient Chinese and at all times: the virtuous, worthy, commendable, perfectible man has always been the man who knew himself to be in bond with God, regardless of whether he was a general or a hermit. And if in his own place he did what man is meant to do, if he achieved the highest possible degree of maturity and worth, then quite as a matter of course he became worthy and important in his action upon others, upon the community and the state.

[86]

Long live diversity, differentiation, and gradation. It is wonderful that there should be many races and peoples, many languages, many mentalities and philosophies. If I hate war, conquest, and annexations and am irreconcilably opposed to them, it is, among other reasons, because so much of what has been fashioned by history, so much that is highly individualized and differentiated in human culture, is destroyed by these dark powers.

[87]

Only at the expense of the self can one live intensely. But the bourgeois values nothing more highly than his self (a rudimentary, underdeveloped one, be it said in passing). Thus he achieves stability and security at the expense of intensity; instead of intoxication with God he attains peace of mind; instead of joy, well-being; instead of freedom, comfort; instead of searing fire, a pleasant temperature. For this reason the bourgeois is essentially a creature of low vitality, anxious, fearing all self-abandonment, easy to govern. Consequently, he has replaced power by the majority, violence by law, responsibility by the ballot.

[88]

The only writers to enjoy some little credit and confidence among discerning readers will soon be those who resolutely forgo the protection conferred by membership in a party, who recognize no master but the truth and their own conscience and are willing to make the sacrifices this may entail. To such men the world conscience may pay some attention, for no one will suspect them of being beneficiaries or fellow travelers of the big power combines. Perhaps a small supranational and nonpartisan spiritual community of this kind is in the making. Even if it consisted of only ten, or five, or three men or women, it would have more moral value than any mass organization of intellectuals with party badges of any kind whatever.

[89]

Twenty-five years later, simple, human ideas are accepted without much resistance by men of good will, but in the meantime history has gone on. Consequently, one can always find a minority of decent men who are ready to stand up for what should have been thought and done twenty-five years before.

[90]

A poet is neither greater nor smaller than a minister, an engineer, or a demagogue, but he is something entirely different. An ax is an ax; with it one can split logs or heads. A clock or a barometer serves for other purposes; if you try to split wood or heads with them, they break, and no one benefits.

[91]

An artist compensates by his work for any deficiencies in his social conduct. The sacrifices he makes to his work—and as a rule they are infinitely greater than what the average good citizen is capable of sacrificing—redound to the benefit of all.

[92]

SOCIETY AND
THE INDIVIDUAL

Society and the Individual

T HE CLOSER TOGETHER people sit, the harder it is for
them to get acquainted.
[93]

The only things that the bourgeois calls "real" are those
that are perceived identically by all or at least by many.
[94]

"A criminal," people say, meaning a man who has done
something that others have forbidden him to do.
[95]

For the good citizen everything is sacrosanct that has to
do with the community, everything that he shares with
many and if possible with all, that never reminds him of
loneliness, of birth and death, or of his innermost self.
[96]

My experience has been this: I have never been attacked
or spat upon for any stupid, insignificant, worthless thing
I have done; every time I have been reviled it has been for
a thought or action that later proved to be right.
[97]

Anyone who has attained a high degree of individuality
must recognize that life is a struggle between sacrifice

and defiance, between recognition of collective values and the rescue of the personality.

[98]

When especially gifted and delicately organized human beings become aware of the cleavages within them, when like every genius they overcome the delusion that the personality is one and come to see themselves as made up of several parts, as bundles of many selves, they need only express this insight and the majority will instantly lock them up, invoke scientific authority, and diagnose schizophrenia, so as to protect mankind from hearing the truth out of the mouths of these unfortunates.

[99]

Nothing makes the multitude angrier than when someone forces them to change their opinion of him.

[100]

Good Lord, what a world this is, where it is impossible to be decent without becoming neurotic!

[101]

What is great or small, important or unimportant? The psychiatrists call a man unbalanced if he reacts sensitively and violently to small upsets, small irritations, small injuries to his dignity, when quite possibly the same individual will bear up bravely under sufferings and shocks that most men find it very hard to take. A man who is insensitive to constant humiliations, who puts up with the most wretched music, the most miserable architecture, the most polluted air without complaint, but who pounds the table and cries bloody murder when he loses so much as a trifle at cards, is regarded as healthy and normal. In taverns I have often seen men of good reputation, generally regarded as perfectly normal and honorable, curse and fume so fanatically, so crudely, so bestially—especially when they felt the need of blaming a fellow player for their losses—that I very much wanted to seek out the nearest psychiatrist and have these unfortunates committed. The truth is that there are many standards, all of which deserve consideration; but I cannot bring myself to hold any of them, including that of science and that of the official morality of the moment, sacred.

[102]

Every man is the center of the world. Around him it seems to revolve willingly; each man and his lifetime are the culmination and climax of history: behind him nations and millennia have died away, and ahead of him there is nothing. The whole gigantic apparatus of history seems to serve only the climactic point of the present moment. To the primitive man every disturbance of this feeling that he is the center, that he is safe on the shore while all others are carried away by the current, is a threat. He refuses to be awakened and enlightened; to him, awakening, thought, and contact with reality are hostile and odious, and with instinctive loathing he turns away from those whom he sees afflicted with states of wakefulness, from seers, questioners, geniuses, prophets, and madmen.

[103]

The same man who is not permitted to transgress the most trifling ethical law for his own benefit is allowed to do anything, to commit the most terrible crimes for collectivity, nation, and fatherland. Then actions that are forbidden in every other context become his heroic duty.

[104]

Each one of us must discover for himself what is permissible and what is forbidden—forbidden to him. It is

31

possible to be a great scoundrel without ever doing anything that is forbidden.

[105]

Those who cannot think or take responsibility for themselves need, and clamor for, a leader.

[106]

The man who is too lazy to think for himself and to be his own judge accommodates himself to existing laws, such as they are. He has it easy.

[107]

What I never wish for, not even in my worst hours, is an average state of mind, halfway between good and bad, a lukewarm, tolerable mean. No, rather an exaggerated swing of the pendulum—rather worse torment, and to make up for it let my happy moments be a little more radiant!

[108]

Man, I believe, is capable of great exaltation and of great baseness; he can rise to the level of a demigod and descend to that of a half-devil; but after doing something great or vile, he always snaps back to his normal state of being. Every swing to demonic savagery is invariably followed by a reaction, by man's inborn yearning for order and moderation.

[109]

The wise are always few. But perhaps they need the masses who enfold and hide them as much as the masses need them.

[110]

In those times of disaster and universal fear, it became apparent that the more a man attunes his life and

32

thought to the spiritual and transpersonal, the more he has learned to venerate, observe, worship, serve, and sacrifice, the more useful he is.

[111]

Men of courage and character always give others a very queasy feeling.

[112]

Where the nobler animals perish, the rabbit conquers; it makes no demands, feels happy, and reproduces prodigiously.

[113]

There is nothing so evil, savage, and cruel in nature as the normal man.

[114]

Today artists and intellectuals are all neurasthenic, or rather, our nerves are not weak at all, but normal, for the truth of the matter is that nerves were made to transmit feelings, and we artists with our sensitive nerves do not regard ourselves as sick, but regard the present-day businessman, technician, or weight lifter, who can feel happy in a modern city with its noise, desolation, and absolutely Hottentot-like commotion, as degenerate.

[115]

A man who has a few notions and does not live in accordance with them is said to have character. He merely intimates in subtle ways that he thinks differently, that he has ideas of his own.

[116]

The same mankind that praises and demands obedience to its arbitrary laws as the supreme virtue reserves its eternal pantheon for those who have defied this demand and preferred to die rather than betray their "self-will."

[117]

What often obstructs or delays my steps in practical life, what looks like hesitation or indecision, may be a weakness, but it is the very opposite of frivolity; it is a strong feeling that man is responsible for everything he does.

[118]

Man has won mastery over this earth, and he is not a good master. But the awakened and the men of good will must nevertheless do their bit, not with doctrines and sermons, but by trying to live meaningfully, each in his own sphere.

[119]

To tell the truth, the only inventions I dislike and distrust are the "useful" ones. All these supposedly useful achievements have an execrable aftermath; they are all so shabby, so ungenerous, so shortsighted; all too soon the motive behind them, the vanity or greed, becomes evident, and everywhere these useful marks of civilization leave behind them a long trail of cruelty, war, death, and hidden misery. Civilization covers the earth with slag and garbage heaps; impressive world fairs and glossy automobile shows are not the only consequence of useful inventions, they also give rise to armies of pale-faced, underpaid miners, to disease and desolation. Man pays for steam engines and turbines with deep scars on his own face and on the face of the earth, with the degradation of worker and employer, with strikes, wars, and other hideous evils. Yet when a man invented the violin or composed the arias in *Figaro*, there was no price at all to pay. Mozart and Mörike cost the world very little. They were

34

as cheap as sunshine; every employee of an engineering
firm costs more.

[120]

Even a superficial man disinclined to thought feels the
age-old need of finding a meaning in his life. When he
ceases to find one, private life falls prey to frenzied self-
seeking and deadly fear.

[121]

It is easy to transform time into money, just as electrical
current can easily be transformed into light and heat.
What is insane and ignoble about that stupidest of all
maxims is the underlying assumption that "money" is a
supreme value.

[122]

It seems to me that for many sufferers from grave mental
illness the sudden loss of their fortunes and the shattering
of their faith in the sanctity of money would be no misfor-
tune at all, but the surest, indeed the only possible salva-
tion. And likewise, it seems to me that it would be most
desirable in this present-day life of ours if the exclusive
cult of work and money could be counteracted by a feel-
ing for the play of the moment, an openness to chance, a
quality we all suffer from the lack of.

[123]

Though we recognize neither "good" nor "bad," right nor
left convictions, we do recognize two kinds of people:
those who try to live according to their convictions and
those who merely keep them in their pockets. That is our
only criterion of judgment.

[124]

When a man feels the need of justifying his life, the crux is not any objective, universally valid level of achievement, but whether he has embodied his inborn essence as fully and purely as possible in his life and actions.

A thousand temptations are always deflecting us from this path, but the most compelling of them all is that deep down we should like to be quite different from what we are, that we try to live up to prototypes and ideals that we cannot, and indeed should not, attain. This temptation is especially strong in highly gifted men and is more dangerous than the vulgar hazards of mere egoism, because it bears an appearance of nobility and morality.

[125]

My task is not to give others what is objectively best, but to go my own way with as much purity and honesty as possible.

[126]

Among men who have become cogs in an organized state and social system, nothing is more unusual and harder to come by than what is reasonable and natural.

[127]

In my experience, the worst enemy and corrupter of man is the tendency—resulting from mental laziness and the desire for peace of mind—to join groups and organizations with set dogmas, be they religious or political.

[128]

It's all a matter of courage. The bravest of us often lose it; then we tend to look for programs, for assurances and guarantees. Courage has need of reason, but it is not reason's child, it springs from deeper strata.

[129]

36

In democratic and intellectually saturated times like ours, it is quite an achievement to discover that there is no such thing as a "normal man" possessing this and that quality and thinking in accordance with this and that Kantian category, but that side by side with the uninteresting herd there are occasional superior men who, though often pathological, are endowed with the possibility of telling the truth, to wit, that the ways of life are inexorable and that every individual stands as a symbol for the whole.

[130]

Although the true saint demands a high degree of asceticism of himself, he is moderate if not indulgent in his demands on the asceticism of others.

[131]

A decent man can't take a single step without making enemies.

[132]

Those who wish to live long must serve. Those who wish to rule do not live long.

[133]

Man in the mass is alien to me and highly suspect. Since the days of my youth, when the masses were still governed by strong ties and repressions, since 1914, we have seen what they are capable of. No, what I love in man is the possibilities of the individual. The thought that mankind might cease to exist the day after tomorrow does not terrify me. But it would grieve me deeply to know that there would be no Goethe, no Mörike, no Tolstoy, no Chekhov, no Renoir or Cézanne tomorrow, or no more of those people who are capable of feeling joy and sadness over Beethoven, Bach, or Hölderlin.

[134]

R E F L E C T I O N S

Money and power are inventions of distrust.

[135]

When we hate someone, it is because we hate some part of ourselves in his image. We don't get excited about anything that is not in ourselves.

[136]

Clarity about one's feelings and about the implications and consequences of one's actions is possible only in good, staunch men who believe in life and never take a step they will be unable to approve of tomorrow and the day after. It is not my good fortune to be one of them; I feel and act like one who does not believe in tomorrow and regards each day as the last.

[137]

We can understand one another, but we can interpret only ourselves.

[138]

The bourgeois attitude has always been present in mankind; it is simply the striving for a balance between the extremes and polarities of human behavior.

[139]

Those who rise higher and are given greater tasks to perform do not gain more freedom but only more responsibility.

[140]

In the Indian view, that is, from the standpoint of the Upanishads and of all pre-Buddhist philosophy, my neighbor is not only "a man like me"; he is I, he is one with me, for the division between him and me, between I and Thou, is delusion, maya. And the entire ethical meaning of brotherly love is contained in this interpretation. For to those who have understood that the world is one, it is obviously absurd that the parts and limbs of this whole should harm one another.

[141]

All degeneration begins with taking big things seriously and regarding it as self-evident that little things should not be taken seriously. To revere humanity but torment one's servants, to hold country or church or party sacred but to do one's daily work poorly and sloppily: that is the beginning of all corruption. Against it there is only one remedy: to disregard for the time being all the supposedly serious and sacred things such as political convictions, philosophy, and patriotism in oneself and others, and instead to give serious attention to the small and smallest things, to the duties of the moment.

[142]

I do not regard the dutiful officer as inferior to the defenseless martyr; each has his place, and his worth is exactly equal to his loyalty and the sacrifices he makes. When an officer does his duty, he has my full respect—if he does not do so, if, though insisting that his soldiers salute him promptly, he thinks first of himself in an emergency, he is a scoundrel. And likewise: if a pacifist preaches nonresistance and nonviolence all his life, but calls for bombs and cannon to defend him when danger threatens, then he too is a scoundrel.

[143]

Though we are prepared to sacrifice our well-being, our comfort, and our life to the nation when it is in danger, this does not mean that we are prepared to sacrifice the spirit itself to the interests of the day, to the generals or the nation. To sacrifice intellectual integrity and the sense of truth to anything else, even to one's country, is treason. The scholar who knowingly says what is untrue, knowingly gives his support to lies and forgeries, is transgressing fundamental, organic laws; furthermore, all momentary appearances to the contrary, he is doing his nation no good but only harm; he is poisoning thought and justice and promoting everything that is hostile and evil.

[144]

It is the duty of us men of the spirit to defy the steamroller of standardization and not to generalize but to differentiate.

[145]

Spirit cannot fight against power, or quality against quantity.

[146]

To hold our tongues when everyone is gossiping, to smile without hostility at people and institutions, to compensate for the shortage of love in the world with more love in small, private matters; to be more faithful in our work, to show greater patience, to forgo the cheap revenge obtainable from mockery and criticism: all these are things we can do.

[147]

Try your level best to find the mode of life that is right for you, even if it means neglecting your "duties." Duties derive all, or at least a good part, of their sanctity from want of courage to fight for one's private life.

[148]

A man who is "ill-adjusted to the world" is always on the point of finding himself. One who is adjusted to the world never finds himself, but gets to be a cabinet minister.

[149]

Every aspiration to instill soul into life is outlawed by the powers that be.

[150]

"Colleagues" like to congregate but seldom get along.

[151]

Don't ask, "Is my attitude toward life the right one?"—to that question there is no answer. Every attitude is as right as every other, all are a part of life. Ask instead, "Since I am as I am, since I have these particular needs and problems which seem to be spared so many others, what must I do in order to bear life, nevertheless, and if possible make something good of it?" If you really listen to your innermost voice, the answer will be something like this: "Since I am as I am, I should neither envy nor despise others for being different. I should not ask whether my being is 'right,' but accept my soul and its needs just as I accept my body, my name, my origins: as something given and inescapable, which I must say yes to and stand up for even if the whole world should oppose it."

[152]

Under usual circumstances we assume that a government official is an excellent citizen, a justified child of God, a properly tagged and useful member of the community, whereas a madman is a poor sick devil, to be tolerated and pitied, but worthless. But then come days or hours, possibly after we have spent a good deal of time with professors or madmen, when the contrary suddenly becomes true: then we discover that the madman is quietly secure in his happiness, a philosopher, a favorite of God, firm in character and content with himself and his faith; the professor or official, on the other hand, seems superfluous, mediocre in character, without personality or individuality, interchangeable.

[153]

41

A rise in the official hierarchy is a step not toward freedom but toward constraint. The greater the power that goes with the office, the stricter the servitude. The stronger the man's character, the more all independence on his part will be frowned on.

[154]

People don't like originals, they prefer to have everything at second hand. They like the new only when it is served up digested and adapted, diminished and prettified.

[155]

Only an individual can do the impossible in the struggle against his natural drives. A community, a nation cannot: they demand to be treated in a purely practical way, with concessions and adjustments.

[156]

Of course, there are many people who find life easier and who seem to be, or actually are, "happier"; people without problems are those who are not strongly individualized.

[157]

All my life I have stood up for the individual, the personality; I do not believe there is any such thing as a universal law that does the individual any good. Laws and prescriptions are not for individuals, but for the many, for herds, nations, and collectivities. True personalities have a harder but also a better time of it: they do not benefit from the protection of the herd, but know the joys of their own imaginations. If they survive the years of their youth, they must bear a heavy responsibility.

[158]

The function of normal men, I saw, was to safeguard and consolidate the existing form of a race, a species, a way of life, so as to provide a firm base, something to fall back on. The function of the visionaries, on the other hand, was to leap and caper, to dream of what had never been thought of before, in order that the fish might some day become a land animal and the ape an anthropoid.

[159]

My work was to defend "private," individual life against the threat of mechanization, war, the state, and mass ideals. I was well aware that it often takes more courage to be merely human, without heroism, than it does to be a hero.

[160]

All appeals to heroism are repressions.

[161]

The spiritual man—and this is my hope for the future—should not become just another successful money-maker. He should not sit at the tables of the rich or share in their luxuries. He should be more or less of an ascetic, but he should not be ridiculed for it; no, he should be respected, and provided as a matter of course with a minimum of material goods, just as in times of monastic culture a monk, though forbidden to have private possessions, was enabled to live and enjoyed a share, proportional to his achievement, in the glory and authority of his order. Spiritual life cannot be directed by an aristocracy; aristocracy is hereditary, and spirit is not, in the physical sense, inherited. A well-ordered spiritual life must revolve around an oligarchy of the most spiritual, but every means of education must be open to the gifted.

[162]

My first article of faith is the unity behind and above the opposites. Of course, I do not deny the possibility of setting up schemas such as "active" and "contemplative," or deny that it is sometimes useful to judge people on the basis of such typologies. There are active and contemplative men. But behind them there is a unity. To my mind, only a man embodying both these opposites can be truly alive and, under favorable circumstances, exemplary. I have no objection either to the relentless worker or to the hermit who contemplates his navel, but I am unable to find either of them interesting, let alone exemplary. The man I look for and hope for is one capable both of living in the world and of being alone, of action as well as meditation. And if in my writings I seem to give the contemplative life precedence over the active life, it is probably because, as I see them, our world and times are full of men who are active, alert, and competent, but incapable of contemplation.

[163]

An airplane and a moon rocket are undoubtedly splendid, gratifying things, but in view of the world's history we find it hard to believe that they can appreciably modify the relations between man and man.

[164]

In the phase of innocence, Pious and Rational battle each other very much like children of different temperaments.

In the second phase, having achieved knowledge, the two contrary poles combat each other with the violence, passion, and tragedy that characterize conflicts between states.

In the third phase, the combatants begin to know each other, no longer as alien beings, but as interdependent. They begin to love and to yearn for one another. From this point, the road leads to possibilities of humanity, whose realization has thus far not been glimpsed by human eyes.

[165]

When we fear someone, it is because we have given this someone power over us.

[166]

The less able I am to believe in our epoch and the more arid and depraved mankind seems in my eyes, the less I look to revolution as the remedy and the more I believe in the magic of love.

[167]

However close human beings may be to one another, there is always a gulf between them that only love can bridge, and even then the bridge is only temporary.

[168]

No one can feel a vibration in others unless he has it in himself.

[169]

"Mankind"—that is, the majority of men—has always been opposed to those who desired the good, for the masses are neither good nor evil; they are above all inert, and hate nothing so much as appeals to their conscience. Development toward higher things, the conquest of egoism and inertia will always be the work of individuals, never of majorities.

[170]

When by hard struggle a personality has broken away from its origins, it is not inclined to surrender its dearly bought freedom and responsibility to any dogma, program, school, trend, or clique.

[171]

THE TASKS OF
THE INDIVIDUAL

The Tasks of the Individual

SAY YES to yourself, to what makes you different, to your feelings, your destiny! There is no other way. Where it leads I don't know, only that it leads to life, to reality, to burning necessity. You may find this unbearable and take your life; that course is open to all, the thought of it often makes one feel better as it does me. But to elude this path by decision, by betrayal of your own destiny and nature, by assimilation to the "normal"—of that you are incapable. You would not succeed for long, and your despair would be greater than it is now.

[172]

Life takes on meaning when we remove it as far as possible from the naïve striving for selfish pleasure, and put it in the service of something. If we take this service seriously, the "meaning" comes of itself.

[173]

As a rule, fear of madness is merely fear of life, of the demands made on us by our development and our instincts. Between naïve instinctual life and what we consciously want and strive to be, there is always a gulf. We cannot bridge it, but I believe we can leap over it, that we can do so continually, many hundreds of times; each time requires courage, and each time we fear to make the leap.

[174]

You say that the quest of the self is less important than finding the right relationship to others. But these are not two different things. Anyone who seeks his authentic self seeks at the same time the norm of all life, for the innermost self is the same in all men. It is God, it is "meaning." That is why the Brahman says of every other being: *"Tat twam asi*—that is thyself!" He knows that he cannot harm another being without harming himself, and that egoism is pointless.

[175]

Only by understanding can we get the better of destiny.

[176]

Some people regard themselves as perfect, but only because they demand little of themselves.

[177]

Man is not a permanent, unchanging creation (this was the ideal of antiquity despite the contradictory intimations of its philosophers); he is rather an experiment and transition, a narrow, dangerous bridge between nature and spirit. His innermost destiny drives him toward the spirit, toward God; his innermost yearning drives him to nature, back to the mother: his life is a fearful wavering between these two powers.

[178]

Nothing is so impossible to describe in words, yet so necessary to impress upon the minds of men as certain things whose existence is neither demonstrable nor probable, but which pious, conscientious men have dwelt with as though they existed and so brought one step closer to being and to the possibility of being born.

[179]

The dignity of man stands and falls with his ability to set himself goals in the realm of the unattainable, and his tragedy lies in the fact that he has the ways and practices of the world against him.

[180]

We should not seek but find, not judge but contemplate and understand, absorb and digest what we have absorbed. We should feel our whole being to be akin and attuned to the whole. Only then can we stand in a true relationship to nature.

[181]

I don't know whether the world has ever been bettered; perhaps it has always been as good and as bad as it is. But this I do know: if ever the world has been bettered, if it has ever been made richer, more alive, happier, more dangerous, more amusing, this has not been the work of reformers, of betterers, but of true self-seekers who have no goal and no purposes, who are content to live and to be themselves.

[182]

Chaos demands to be recognized and experienced before letting itself be converted into a new order.

[183]

Every destiny, however much it may seem to be determined by certain situations, bears within it all the possibilities of life and transformation implicit in the man himself. And the more childhood, gratitude, and capacity for love we have, the greater these will be.

[184]

Time and time again we cling to the things we have learned to love; we call this fidelity, but it is only inertia.

[185]

51

Practice ought to be the consequence of thought, not the other way round.

[186]

I hold that I am not responsible for the meaningfulness or meaninglessness of life, but that I am responsible for what I do with my own unique life.

[187]

When fate comes to a man from outside, it fells him as an arrow fells a deer. When it comes to him from within, from his innermost being, it strengthens him and makes him into a god.

[188]

If you know that your struggle will be unsuccessful, that will not make your life shallow and stupid. It will be much more so if you struggle for something good and ideal and think you are sure to attain it.

[189]

Yes, there is such a thing as peace, but there is no peace that dwells in us eternally and never leaves us. There is only a peace that must be won time and time again by unceasing struggle, that must be won each day anew.

[190]

Every conflict that has not been suffered to the end and resolved will recur.

[191]

God does not send us despair in order to kill us; he sends it in order to awaken us to new life.

[192]

Undoubtedly it is very hard to live with lasting physical

pain. Men of heroic character resist pain, try to deny it, and grit their teeth after the manner of the Roman Stoics. But attractive as this attitude is, we are inclined to doubt whether one can really conquer pain. For my part, I have been most successful in living with pain, not when I have resisted it but when I have given in to it, as one gives in to drunkenness or to an adventure.

[193]

Every attempt to take culture, the human spirit and its demands, seriously and to live by it leads invariably to despair. Salvation then comes from the realization that we have gone too far in objectifying subjective experiences and states. Of course, such experiences of salvation are no guarantee against new despair. But they promote the belief that all despair can be overcome from within.

[194]

We must become so alone, so utterly alone, that we withdraw into our innermost self. It is a way of bitter suffering. But then our solitude is overcome, we are no longer alone, for we find that our innermost self is the spirit, that it is God, the indivisible. And suddenly we find ourselves in the midst of the world, yet undisturbed by its multiplicity, for in our innermost soul we know ourselves to be one with all being.

[195]

Loneliness is the way by which destiny endeavors to lead man to himself.

[196]

Conscience has nothing to do with morality or law; it can enter into the most terrible, the most deadly conflicts with both, but it is infinitely strong, stronger than inertia, stronger than self-seeking, stronger than vanity.

[197]

No precious jewel is so invulnerably beautiful that habit and lovelessness cannot take away its luster; accordingly, it seems to me, we should strive for the art of devoting the same reverence and love to the customary beauties around us as we do so readily to those that are far away.

[198]

Opinions interest me only when they lead to deeds and sacrifices. Consequently, I very much prefer a man who thinks the opposite from myself, but who appeals to me and impresses me as a man, to one who agrees with me but whom I suspect of being a coward and a windbag.

[199]

Reality is what we cannot under any circumstances be satisfied with, what we must not under any circumstances worship or admire, for it is accident, a waste product of life. The only way we can change it is by denying it, by showing that we are stronger than it is.

[200]

Under no circumstances can we, who from art, nature, or the sciences have acquired a feeling for quality and undertaken to foster it, be under obligation to foster quantity and, either in the Western or in the Eastern way, promote the fallacy that human problems can be solved in the same way as mathematical ones. We must work for the values in which we really believe, even if we can do so only in the most restricted sphere.

[201]

It is not crucial for the value and growth of my self that I should at all times be conscious of the things that are important to me, but only that I maintain good, easy, fluid relations between the spheres of consciousness and of the unconscious. We are not thinking machines, but organisms.

[202]

We must begin not with political methods and forms of government, but at the beginning, with the building of the personality, if we wish again to have minds and men capable of securing our future.

[203]

It is easier to die for a cause than to live for it.

[204]

Man is not determinate, clearly defined once and for all; he is something in process of development, an experiment, an intimation of the future, the quest and yearning of nature for new forms and new possibilities.

[205]

Virtue is obedience. The question is only: *Whom* are we to obey? For self-will is also obedience. But all the other virtues, the virtues that are so highly esteemed and praised, consist in obedience to man-made laws. Self-will is the only virtue that takes no account of these laws. A self-willed man obeys a different law, the one law I hold absolutely sacred—the law in himself, his own "will."

[206]

What repels me exists for me no less than what I love. But what I don't know and don't want to know, what leaves me indifferent, what is unrelated to me and does not speak to me, does not exist for me—and the more of it there is, the lower I myself stand in the scale of being.

[207]

Deeds—are never done by one who first asks, "What should I do?"

[208]

All cultural achievement in this world has been brought ideals are threatened. But when a new ideal, a new, possibly dangerous and terrifying impulse of growth knocks at the door, no one is home.

[209]

All cultural achievement in this world has been brought about by men who conceived ideals and hopes far exceeding what was possible at the moment.

[210]

The greater a man's education and the privileges he has enjoyed, the greater should be his sacrifices in time of need.

[211]

One who accepts a calling is not only accepting a gift and a command, he is also taking a kind of guilt upon himself, just as when a soldier is singled out from among his comrades to become an officer; the greater his sense of guilt toward his comrades, the worthier he will be of his promotion.

[212]

To think is to discern causes; this alone transforms feelings into insights that are not lost, but take on substance and radiance.

[213]

Don't say that any emotion is insignificant, that any emotion is unworthy! They are all good, very good, even hatred, even envy, jealousy, cruelty. We live by nothing else than our poor, beautiful, magnificent emotions, and every emotion we disregard is a star that we extinguish.

[214]

From everything that man has desired he has been separated only by time—by time, that fantastic invention. It is one of the props, one of the crutches, we must throw away if we want to be free.

[215]

The more we demand of ourselves, or the more the task in hand demands of us, the more dependent we are on meditation as a source of strength, on the continually renewed reconciliation of spirit and soul . . .

All the truly great men in the history of the world have either known how to meditate or unconsciously found the way to the place where meditation leads us. The rest, even the strongest and most gifted, have all failed and been defeated in the end, because their task or ambitious dream so took possession of them, so possessed them that they lost the faculty of detachment from current contingencies.

[216]

My life, as I see it, should be a transcending, a progression from stage to stage; one sphere after another should be traversed and left behind, just as a piece of music completes and leaves behind it theme after theme, tempo after tempo, never weary, always awake, always fully alert to the present. In connection with the experience of waking, I had noticed that such stages and spheres exist, and that the end of each period of life always carries a tonality of fading and dying, which leads the way to a new sphere, an awakening, a fresh start.

[217]

When a man is looking for something, it easily comes about that his mind sees only what he is looking for—that he can find nothing, assimilate nothing, because he can think only of what he is looking for, because he has an aim, because he is possessed by his aim. To seek is to have an aim. To find is to be free and open, to have no aim.

[218]

Patience is the most difficult thing of all and the only thing that is worth learning. All nature, all growth, all peace, everything that flowers and is beautiful in the world depends on patience, requires time, silence, trust, and faith in long-term processes which far exceed any single lifetime, which are accessible to the insight of no one person, and which in their totality can be experienced only by peoples and epochs, not by individuals.

[219]

To each man life sets a different, unique task. Consequently there is no such thing as an innate, predetermined incapacity for life; merely by accepting the place in life that he himself did not choose and trying to make the most of it, even the weakest and poorest of men can, in his own way, lead a worthy, authentic life and mean something to others. That is true humanity; it always diffuses a noble, healing power, even when the man to whom the task has fallen is a poor devil with whom one would not wish to change places.

[220]

The knowledge or belief that all knowledge is fragmentary should stop no one from going on with his building and attaining the possible.

[221]

The best weapons against the infamies of life are courage, an independent mind, and patience. Courage strengthens, the independent mind amuses, and patience gives peace.

[222]

As a rule, the bad, stupid periods of my life have agreed with me more than the reasonable and seemingly successful ones. I must have patience, not reason. I must sink my roots deeper, not shake my branches.

[223]

We require still another education besides the intellectual. We have submitted to the ethic of the Order, not so as to bend our intellectually active life into a vegetative dream life, but on the contrary, so as to make ourselves capable of the highest intellectual achievement. We should not escape from the *vita activa* to the *vita contemplativa,* nor conversely, but move back and forth between the two, make ourselves at home in both, participate in both.

[224]

Life is meaningless, cruel, stupid, and nevertheless magnificent—it does not make fun of man (for that requires intelligence), but concerns itself with man no more than with the earthworm. To suppose that man in particular is a whim and cruel game of nature is a fallacy that man himself has thought up because he takes himself too seriously. First of all, we must recognize that we men have no harder time of it than birds or ants, that actually our life is easier and more beautiful. We must take the cruelty of life and the inexorability of death into ourselves, not by moaning, but by experiencing our despair to the full. Only then, only when we have taken all the cruelty or meaninglessness of nature into ourselves, can

we begin to confront this brutal meaninglessness and to
force a meaning on it. That is the highest achievement
man is capable of, and it is all he is capable of. Everything
else is done better by animals.

Most men do not suffer from meaninglessness, any
more than the earthworm does. But precisely the few who
do suffer and look for meaning are the meaning of man-
kind.

[225]

Problems do not exist in order to be solved; they are
merely the poles that engender the tension necessary for
life.

[226]

Every strong man invariably achieves what an authentic
drive leads him to strive for.

[227]

If not for the beast within us we would be castrated
angels.

[228]

Every man, insofar as he is a person with a face, has his
allotted, inborn destiny. He enacts and suffers this al-
lotted destiny so naturally that it often looks as if he had
chosen it on purpose.

[229]

Man, as conceived by God and as seen by the literature
and wisdom of the peoples for some thousands of years,
was created with a capacity for taking pleasure even in
things that are of no use to him, with an organ for the
beautiful. Spirit and senses partake equally in his enjoy-
ment of beauty, and as long as man is able amid the

tribulations and dangers of his life to enjoy such things—nature's play of colors, a painting, the voice of the storm, of the sea, of man-made music; as long as he is able, under his surface needs and interests, to see and feel the world as a whole, to derive joy and wisdom, amusement and sympathy from the thousands of relationships, correspondences, analogies, and echoes that speak to us eternally from things great and small—the tilt of a playing kitten's head, the modulations of a sonata, the touching look in the eyes of a dog, a great poem; as long as man has this capacity, he will know how to deal with what is problematic in his existence and continually to find new meaning in his life, for "meaning" is precisely the unity of the manifold, the power of the human spirit to sense unity and harmony in the world's confusion.

[230]

I have always believed, and I still believe, that whatever good or bad fortune may come our way we can always give it meaning and transform it into something of value. Neither for myself nor for others shall I ever abandon this belief.

[231]

Intelligence is noble and beneficial only when it serves the truth; once it betrays the truth, once it casts off reverence, becomes venal and opportunistic, it becomes a power for evil, far worse than animal, instinctive bestiality, which always retains some of the innocence of nature.

[232]

The sufferings of the world should find us indestructible in our innermost being, but not armored against them by some sort of perfect philosophy.

[233]

We are the playthings not of a blind power outside us, but of the gifts, weaknesses, and other hereditary factors that a man brings into the world with him. The aim of a meaningful life is to hear the call of this inner voice and as far as possible to follow it. The essential, then, is to know yourself; this does not mean to judge and try to change yourself, but to do your utmost to give your life the form foreshadowed by your intimations.

[234]

Your theoretical question as to whether a human life is worth more than the *St. Matthew Passion* is frivolous, and the answer to which you incline is dangerous. A man without culture, without history, without art is less desirable than any animal, and to hold that sheer life is worth more than history and art is to think in terms of "blood and soil," an attitude which, as we know, has no regard whatever for human life and its preservation. A human individual is not a higher value in himself, but only as possibility, as a way to the spirit.

[235]

One can always become innocent again provided one faces up to one's suffering and guilt and suffers them to the end, instead of blaming them on others.

[236]

On the whole I am distrustful of heroism and also of stoicism. In my own life, except for a few rare instances, I have held that my shortest way through the world of pain was the way that led straight through pain.

[237]

Virtues, like talents, are dangerous, though in specific situations they are useful hypertrophies, rather like goose

62

livers forced to enormous size. Since I can develop no talent or virtue in myself without diverting the requisite psychic energy from other impulses, every highly developed virtue involves a specialization at the expense of other aspects of life that are repressed and left to languish, just as it is possible to blow up the intellect at the expense of the senses, or feeling at the expense of reason.

[238]

Feel with all the suffering of the world, but don't turn your strength to matters in which you are helpless; expend it on your neighbor whom you can help, love, and cheer.

[239]

Our mission is to gain true discernment of the contraries, first as contraries, but then as poles of a unity.

[240]

It is not our task to come closer to one another any more than sun and moon or land and sea will ever meet. Our goal is to know one another, to see and learn to revere the other for what he is: our own counterpart and complement.

[241]

The winner is always he who can love, be indulgent, and forgive, not he who self-righteously condemns.

[242]

We kill when we close our eyes to poverty, affliction, or infamy. We kill when, because it is easier, we countenance or even pretend to approve of atrophied social, political, educational, and religious institutions, instead of resolutely combating them. Just as a consistent socialist

looks on property as theft, so those who hold consistently
to our kind of faith regard all contempt for human life, all
cruelty and indifference as tantamount to killing. And not
only things present can be killed, but the things of the
future as well.

[243]

Leadership means little to us, service everything. Before
all other virtues, we cultivate reverence, but we do not
give reverence to persons.

[244]

There is no other way to growth and fulfillment than the
most perfect unfolding of one's own essence. "Be thyself"
is the ideal law, at least for a young man; there is no other
way to truth and development.

This way is made difficult by many moral and other
obstacles. The world would rather see us adapted and
weak than independent, and for every man who is indi-
vidualized beyond the average, this is a source of lifelong
struggle. Each man must decide for himself, according to
his own resources and his own needs, how far to submit
to conventions or to defy them. When he throws the
conventions, the demands of family, state, collectivity to
the winds, it must be in full awareness that he is doing so
at his own peril. There is no objective way of measuring
the amount of danger a man is capable of taking on him-
self. Every excess, every overstepping of one's own mea-
sure must be paid for; no man can go too far in indepen-
dence or in adaptation with impunity.

[245]

Pleasant as it is to adapt oneself to one's environment and
to the spirit of the times, the pleasures of integrity are
greater and more lasting.

[246]

We should devote ourselves to the needs and problems of the day only if we are prepared to take a partisan stand and commit ourselves entirely. Since I know of no party whose aims I can fully approve, this course is not open to me.

[247]

The world will not get ahead any faster if you turn poets into demagogues, philosophers into ministers. It will get ahead wherever a man does what he is here for, what his nature demands of him, what he consequently does gladly and well.

[248]

If here and now, in the face of today's difficulties and requirements, we behave with a certain amount of human decency, it is possible that the future, too, will be human.

[249]

A man of character reveals it most clearly and purely when, removed from his usual sphere of life, he finds himself confronting something new.

[250]

A profound desire to travel is no different and no less poignant than the dangerous yearning to think without fear, to turn the world on its head, and to obtain answers from all things, persons, and events. It cannot be appeased by plans or books; it demands more and costs more, we must put our heart's blood into it.

[251]

EDUCATION
AND SCHOOLS

Education and Schools

True education is not education for any purpose; like all striving for perfection, it carries its purpose in itself. Just as the striving for physical strength, dexterity, and beauty serves no ultimate aim, such as to make us rich, famous, and powerful, but is its own reward, since it enhances our life-feeling and self-confidence, since it makes us happier and more resilient and gives us a greater feeling of assurance and health, so the striving for "education," that is, for improvement of the mind, is not an arduous journey toward any definite goal, but a gratifying and fortifying broadening of our consciousness, an enrichment of our possibilities of life and happiness. Accordingly, true education, like true physical culture, is at once a fulfillment and a spur; always at the goal and never stopping to rest, it is a journey in the infinite, a participation in the movement of the universe, a living in timelessness. Its purpose is not to enhance particular abilities; rather, it helps us to give meaning to our lives, to interpret the past, to be fearless and open toward the future.

[252]

I have never set much store by formal education, that is, I have always had serious doubts whether a man can be in any way changed or improved by it. Instead, I have had a certain confidence in the gently persuasive power of the beautiful, of art and literature, which, for my own part, did far more than any public or private schooling to mold me and make me curious about the world of the spirit.

[253]

No one can see and understand anything in someone else that he has not experienced in himself.

[254]

The truth is lived, not taught.

[255]

A schoolmaster would rather have ten notorious dunces in his class than one genius, and come to think of it, he's right, for his job is to turn out not extravagant minds but good Latinists, mathematicians, and God-fearing citizens. Which suffers more at the hands of the other, the teacher at the hands of the pupil or conversely, which of the two is a worse tyrant, a worse tormenter, and which of the two it is who corrupts and desecrates parts of the other's soul and life is a question I am unable to ponder without bitterness.

[256]

The question of schools is the only modern cultural question that I take seriously and sometimes get worked up about. In me school destroyed a great deal, and I know of few men of any stature who cannot say the same. All I learned there was Latin and lying.

[257]

Our teachers demanded of us virtues they themselves did not possess; consequently the history they set before us was a swindle invented by grownups for the purpose of belittling us and humiliating us.

[258]

In that amusing subject they called history, our teachers taught us that the world had always been governed, guided, and changed by men who made their own law and broke with the traditional laws, and they told us that these men deserved to be admired. But this was just as much of a lie as everything else we were taught, for when one of us, with good or bad intent, summoned up the courage to protest against any regulation, or even against an absurd custom or fashion, he was neither admired nor pointed out as an example, but punished, ridiculed, and crushed under the cowardly weight of the teacher's authority.

[259]

When it came to poets, it was the same as with heroes and all other beautiful, high-hearted, extraordinary figures and undertakings: in the past they were glorious, all the schoolbooks were full of their praises, but in reality, in the present, they were hated. It looked as though teachers had been trained and engaged precisely to prevent children from growing up into fine, free men who might do great and glorious deeds.

[260]

Man as nature made him is incalculable, inscrutable, and hostile. He is a torrent bursting forth from an unknown mountain, a virgin forest without pathways or order. And just as a forest must be thinned and cleaned up and fenced in, so man in the state of nature must be broken, defeated, and fenced in by schools; it is their function to transform him, in accordance with principles approved by the sovereign authorities, into a useful member of society, and to awaken in him those qualities that will be raised to perfection by the vigilant discipline of the barracks.

[261]

Jesus was twelve years old when he shamed the doctors in the temple. We all of us at the age of twelve shamed our doctors and teachers; we were more intelligent than they, more inspired than they, more courageous than they.

[262]

So much of what a child does is put down as misconduct merely because it is disturbing to parents, but the child is only doing what comes natural to him; to him it is innocent and his conscience is untroubled.

[263]

Only the thinking that we act on has any value. You knew your "permissible world" was only half the world, but you tried to suppress the other half in yourself, as the parsons and teachers do.

[264]

Punch filial piety in the nose—that is one of the things we have to do if we are to get away from our mother's apron strings.

[265]

When we were children, grownups were at great pains to "break our will," as the pious pedagogy of the day put it. They did indeed break and ruin a good deal of what was in us, but not our will, not the unique inborn spark that made us outsiders and eccentrics.

[266]

When I was about fifteen, one of our teachers disconcerted us by saying that suicide was the worst possible act of moral cowardice. Until then I had rather tended to believe that it required a certain courage, a certain defiance and suffering, and my feeling toward suicides had been one of respect mingled with horror. Consequently, the teacher's statement, delivered with the assurance of an axiom, shook me for the moment. It left me speechless, without answer, for it seemed to have all logic and morality on its side. But I was not shaken for long; I soon recovered my faith in my own feelings and ideas, and ever since then I have thought suicides estimable, congenial, and somehow, though in a gruesome kind of way, outstanding, examples of a human suffering beyond the scope of that teacher's imagination, of a courage and defiance that I can only love. And, to tell the truth, all the suicides I have known, for all their problematic characters, have been worthy, above-average men. In addition to the courage to put a bullet through their heads, they had the courage and defiance to arouse the dislike and contempt of schoolteachers and moralists. This could only increase my sympathy.

[267]

The educated man knows and has principles. He respects any number of things, which at bottom attract him very little, and forgoes others to which he would be attracted if his education had not built up inhibitions.

[268]

In my generation, I believe, many more human lives have been bungled by too much throttling and repression of their instincts than by the contrary. In some of my books, for this reason, I have made myself the advocate and friend of the repressed instinctual life—but never to the detriment of the lofty imperatives formulated by the philosophers and the religions. And indeed, we do not propose to indulge our savage, lawless instincts at the expense of kindness, love, and humanity. Rather, we try to steer a course between the demands of nature and those of the spirit; not a rigid middle course, but a flexible one, varying with each individual, in which freedom and law alternate like inhalation and exhalation.

[269]

The reasonable man rationalizes the world and does it violence. He tends to be grimly serious. He is an educator.

[270]

Knowledge has no worse enemy than wanting to know, than learning.

[271]

In my experience, the only conscience that can be aroused and fired is one that is already awake.

[272]

There are readers who get along all their lives with a dozen books and are nevertheless authentic readers. And there are others who have imbibed everything and are able to join in a conversation about anything, yet all their effort has been in vain. For education presupposes something to be educated: to wit, a character, a personality. Where that is lacking, where there is no substance and education operates in the void, as it were, knowledge may result, but not love or life. Reading without love, knowledge without reverence, education without heart are among the worst sins against the spirit.

[273]

An educated man is merely more educated, by no means more intelligent, than the common people.

[274]

Whether you become a teacher, a scholar, or a musician, revere the "meaning," but don't suppose it can be taught.

By trying to teach the "meaning," philosophers of history have corrupted half of world history.

[275]

Judgments are of value when they affirm. Every negative, disparaging judgment, even when based on sound observation, becomes false the moment it is uttered. Three-quarters of what people say about each other consists of such "judgments." When I say that someone is repugnant to me, that is an honest statement. It leaves anyone who hears me free to blame this repugnance either on me or on the other fellow. But when I say that someone is vain or avaricious or drinks, I do wrong. Anyone can be annihilated by this kind of judgment. Jean Paul becomes a beer drinker, Feuerbach a dandy, Hölderlin a madman. But does this tell us anything about them, does it give us any insight? You might just as well say: The earth is a planet with fleas on it. This kind of "truth" is the quintessence of all falsehood. We are really telling the truth only when we affirm and give recognition. Though the pointing out of "faults" may sound ever so witty, it is not judgment but gossip.

[276]

All culture and intellectual life has two functions. One is to give certainty and encouragement to the many, to comfort them, to give meaning to their lives. The second is more mysterious and no less important: to enable the few, the great minds of tomorrow and the day after, to mature, to shelter and care for their beginnings, to give them air to breathe.

[277]

Young people find in my writings a spur to individuality, whereas teachers strive for the exact opposite, the greatest possible uniformity, the normalization of young minds. This is quite as it should be. To understand that both functions, mine which seduces to individualism and that of the schools which tends toward normalcy, are necessary complements to one another, that they go hand in hand like inhalation and exhalation and all other bipolar processes, and to feel lovingly at one with our adversary even when it is necessary to oppose him, requires a little wisdom and a little reverence and piety. These are qualities which today can no more be taken for granted in teachers than in anyone else. Today, and perhaps for a long time to come, the world is in the hands of the *Grands Simplificateurs*, and in all likelihood a recovery from this state of affairs will not be possible until after a catastrophe, the beginnings of which we have been observing since 1914.

[278]

RELIGION AND
THE CHURCH

Religion and the Church

ONE RELIGION is about as good as another. In every one of them a man has the possibility of becoming wise or of practicing the stupidest idolatry. But almost all mankind's true knowledge has been amassed in the religions, especially in the mythologies. Every mythology is "false," unless we look at it with piety; but every mythology is a key to the heart of the world; they all know of ways to transform self-idolatry into divine worship.

[279]

To my mind the humanistic ideal is no more commendable than the religious ideal; nor among the religions can I give precedence to one over another. It would be impossible for me to belong to any church, because the churches lack broadness and freedom of spirit, because every church regards itself as the best and holds those outside it to be in error.

The way to the churches is easy to find, the doors are wide open, and there is no lack of propaganda.

[280]

The wisdom of all peoples is one and the same; there are not two or more wisdoms, there is only one. My only objection to religions and churches is their tendency to intolerance: neither Christian nor Mohammedan is likely to admit that his faith, though holy, is neither privileged

79

nor patented, but a brother to all the other faiths in which the truth tries to make itself manifest.

[281]

We are transient, we are in process of becoming, we are possibilities; for us there is no perfection, no absolute being. But where we move from potency to act, from possibility to realization, we partake of true being, we come one step closer to the perfect and divine. This is self-realization.

[282]

When a man tries, with the gifts bestowed on him by nature, to fulfill himself, he is doing the highest thing he can do, the only thing that has any meaning.

[283]

Nor should you yearn for a perfect doctrine; yearn, rather, for perfection of yourself. The godhead is in you, not in concepts and books.

[284]

There can be no noble, no higher life without the knowledge of devils and demons and without a constant struggle against them.

[285]

Atheism is merely the negation of something that never had a substantial but only a verbal existence.

[286]

Every religion tinged with reform makes feelings of inferiority into a cult; a suggestion of this is also perceptible in Buddhism.

[287]

Piety is nothing other than trust. Trust is to be found in the simple, the healthy, the innocent: in children and savages.

[288]

One who says no to himself cannot say yes to God.

[289]

The way to innocence, to the uncreated, to God does not lead backward, but forward, not to the wolf or to the child, but deeper and deeper into guilt, further and further in the direction of manhood.

[290]

Faith and doubt go hand in hand, they are complementaries. One who never doubts will never truly believe.

[291]

A pious man easily falls in love with mythologies.

[292]

The essential, I believe, is not what faith a man has, but that he should have one.

[293]

Comparable to Jesus is any man who, touched by one of the magical truths, ceases to distinguish between thinking and living and, thereby estranged from those around him, becomes the adversary of all.

[294]

I regard the confusion of inner with outward tasks, of the soul with politics, as one of the most tragic themes in history—this because I do not believe in a kingdom of God that is anywhere else than where Jesus told the disciples; that is, within us.

[295]

In the political thinking of advanced peoples nationalism is a thing of the past; in all the religions a childish faith in the sole validity of one's own faith is still prevalent.

[296]

I believe that for all its patent absurdities life nevertheless has a meaning. I resign myself to being unable to find this ultimate meaning with my reason, but I am prepared to serve it even if it means sacrificing myself.

Such faith cannot be commanded, we cannot force it on ourselves. We can only experience it. Those who cannot do that seek their faith in the church or in science or in patriotism or socialism, in some quarter where there are ready-made moralities, programs, and prescriptions.

[297]

Youth leaves scars on the soul of almost every halfway differentiated human being. Apart from psychoanalysis, there are many means of dealing with them. One of these is religion, and even such a substitute for religion as membership in a political party is another.

[298]

We insist that life must have a meaning—but it can have no more meaning than we ourselves are able to give it. Because individuals can do this only imperfectly, the religions and philosophies have tried to supply a comforting answer to the question.

These answers all amount to the same thing: love alone can give life meaning. In other words: the more capable we are of loving, and of giving ourselves, the more meaning there will be in our lives.

[299]

With regard to pessimism or optimism or philosophies in general, a man who is alive, and especially an artist, cannot readily commit himself to any one. I at least cannot, nor do I ever feel the need of being right; I take pleasure in diversity, including that of opinions and faiths. This prevents me from being a good Christian, for I believe neither that God had only one son nor that belief in that one son is the only way to God or beatitude. Piety always appeals to me, whereas I dislike authoritarian theologies with their claim to exclusive validity.

[300]

An ethical system can be the product of a religion, but never can a religion be built up from an ethic. For the higher of the two is religion. I do not believe that any religion began with ethics, whereas most philosophies began with religion.

[301]

If mankind were an individual, it could be helped by "pure" Christianity; then it would surely be possible to exorcise the beast and the demon. But this is not the case. The "pure" religions are for a small elite; the people need magic and mythology. I do not believe in a process of upward development. Time and time again, pure individuals and saviors rise up from the dull mass of mankind and are not revered by the many until after they have been crucified and made into gods.

[302]

I believe that the elite of Christianity will always be those who tend to find its formulations shallow. Nevertheless I am convinced that the "new" order they long for is the same as the old and that the old formulations regain their living magic insofar as the seeker is prepared to take formulas as symbols.

[303]

If His churches and priests were like Christ Himself, there would be no need of poets.

[304]

I have chosen the way of the egoist or religious man, and regard outward duties as secondary to our duties to our own souls. I feel more strongly than ever that my soul is a small part of all human development and that fundamentally the slightest quiver within us is as important as war and peace in the outside world.

[305]

Each man is not only himself; he is also the unique, very special, and in every case important point where the world's manifestations intersect, only once in this particular way and never again. For this reason the history of each man is important, eternal, divine, and for this reason every man, as long as he is in any way alive and fulfills the will of nature, is a marvelous thing, worthy of the utmost attention. In each man the spirit is embodied, in each man the creature suffers, in each man the Saviour is crucified.

[306]

We put much too narrow a definition on personality! Our personality, we tend to believe, is only that part of ourselves which we regard as individual, as deviating from the norm. But we, each and all of us, contain within us the entire history of the world, and just as our body records man's genealogy as far back as the fish and then some, so our soul encompasses everything that has ever lived in human souls. All gods and devils that have ever existed are within us, as possibilities, as desires, as solutions. If mankind were to die out except for one halfway gifted child, who had been taught nothing, that child would rediscover all history; it would create gods, de-

mons, paradises, commandments and prohibitions, the
Old and New Testaments.

[307]

The faith that we take seriously is not a faith in ourself,
in our opinions, our courage, loyalty, etc., but a faith in
the grace that may possibly await us, that we can never
deserve but always hope for. What made the frail Peter
into a rock can make a rock of every man. That is what
we should believe. As for the rest, namely, that we men
are half animals, capable of every kind of stupidity and
cowardice, we don't have to believe that, because we know
it; one glance at daily life, at history, at our own lives and
hearts suffices. This dismal knowledge is offset by a
liberating faith, which for this reason is "higher than all
reason."

[308]

I regard piety as the best virtue we can have, worth more
than all talents. By piety I do not mean the cultivation of
solemn feelings in an individual soul; most of all, I mean
the individual's reverence for the world as a whole, for
nature, for his fellow men, a feeling of participation and
co-responsibility.

[309]

I believe that we do not end in nothingness, and I believe
that our work and concern for what we thought good and
right has not been in vain. But in what ways the whole
inspires and continually sustains us parts—on that score I
can spin fantasies now and then, but not accept a dog-
matic opinion. Faith is trust, not the desire to know.

[310]

My whole life has been governed by the quest for a bond
of devotion, for religion. It has never crossed my mind

that I might be able to discover anything on the order of a new religion for myself and others, a new formulation or possible bond. What I do believe is that I must stand fast at my post, that even if I am driven to despair of my times and myself I must preserve my reverence for life and for the possibility of giving it meaning, even if in this belief I should find myself alone and make myself ridiculous. To this creed I hold fast, not in the hope of making anything better for the world or for myself, but simply because I cannot live without some sort of reverence, without devotion to a God.

[311]

Every true Protestant resists his own church as he does every other, because his nature bids him attach more importance to what man can become than to what he is.

[312]

Both in a Christian and in a psychological sense, a "guilty conscience" is an indication of a living and healthy, though troubled, conscience.

[313]

Our conscience is a high authority, but I doubt whether it is always the voice of God; and it is undoubtedly fortunate that this authority is opposed by another, the pure life drive.

[314]

Repentance alone is of no help; grace cannot be bought with repentance; it cannot in any way be bought.

[315]

Like art and poetry, the religions and myths are an attempt on the part of mankind to express in images the ineffable, which you are trying in vain to translate into shallow rationality.

[316]

Times of transition are marked by the emergence of strange new gods, who always look more like devils. What has hitherto been reasonable becomes meaningless; what was hitherto insane becomes positive and hopeful; all dividing lines seem to be effaced, all evaluation impossible; these are the times of the demiurge, who is neither good nor evil, neither god nor devil, but only a creator, only a destroyer, only a blind primordial force. Such a moment, when the world seems to be coming to an end, is, for the individual, shattering experience, miracle, conversion. It is a moment of lived paradox, the flashing moment when the opposite poles meet, when dividing lines vanish, and norms melt away. It may be that ethical and social orders will go under, but the event itself is the most vital that can be conceived of.

[317]

The myths of the Bible, like all myths, are worthless for us unless we venture to interpret them for ourselves and our times. But then they can mean a great deal to us.

[318]

No good can come of deploring war, technology, money-madness, nationalism, etc. We must replace the idols of our time with a faith.

[319]

Freedom from conventions is not synonymous with inner freedom. For the higher type of men, life in a world without rigidly formulated faith is not easier, but far more difficult, because they themselves must create and choose the obligations that will govern their lives.

[320]

In speaking with members of a church or religious community, I am careful to say nothing that might undermine their faith. For most men it is a very good thing to belong to a church and faith. The first experience of those who break away is a loneliness that makes a good many of them hanker for the old community. Only much later will they discover that they have entered into a new community, great but invisible, which encompasses all peoples and all religions. They will be poorer in all dogmatic, national goods, but richer in brotherhood with the souls of all epochs, nations, and languages.

[321]

All living knowledge (i.e., knowledge that has a direct effect on life) has but one object. It is known by many and expressed in a thousand ways, but it is always the One Truth. It is the knowledge of what is alive in us, of the secret magic, the secret godliness that each of us bears within him: the knowledge that starting from this innermost point it is possible to transcend all the pairs of opposites. The Hindu calls it Atman; the Chinese, Tao; the Christian, grace.

[322]

Grace, or the Tao, surrounds us always. It is the light and it is God Himself. Whenever we are open for a moment, it enters into us, into every child, into every wise man.

[323]

The pious man sees the world in terms of myth and often, for this reason, does not take it seriously enough. He is always somewhat inclined to play. He does not educate children but rejoices in their happiness.

[324]

Christmas is an epitome, a poison chamber of all bourgeois sentimentalities and hypocrisies, an occasion for wild orgies on the part of industry and commerce, for garish luxury displays in the department stores; it smells of lacquered tin, of pine needles and phonographs, of exhausted, secretly cursing delivery boys and postmen, of embarrassed festivities centering on decorated fir trees, of special supplements bursting with advertisements, in short, of a thousand things that are bitterly hateful and repugnant to me, things that would only make me laugh or leave me indifferent if they did not so blatantly abuse the name of the Saviour and our tenderest childhood memories.

[325]

God: the One Spirit above all images and multiplicities.

[326]

KNOWLEDGE AND
CONSCIOUSNESS

Knowledge and Consciousness

K NOWLEDGE has no ultimate goals; its progress is merely a greater differentiation in the questions raised.

[327]

To mere reason the world always looks two-dimensional.

[328]

Knowledge is action. Knowledge is experience. It has no permanence. The time of its being is the moment.

[329]

Sensory impressions are more fertile soil for memories than the best systems and methods of thought.

[330]

Those whose chief concern is thought can go far in it, but they mistake water for the dry land and one day they will drown in it.

[331]

The more sharply and unswervingly we pursue a thesis, the more irresistibly it will call for its antithesis.

[332]

The most central purpose of my life is this: to replace the crude invisibility under the magic hood by the invisibility

of the wise man, who in knowing always remains un-
known.

[333]

The man whom I look at with fear, with hope, with
desire, with purposes, with demands, is not a man but
only a blurred mirror of my will. Knowingly or unknow-
ingly, I look at him with questions that narrow him down
and falsify him: Is he accessible or proud? Does he
respect me? Can I borrow money from him? Does he
know anything about art? We look at most of the people
we approach with a thousand such questions, and are
given credit for psychology and knowledge of human
nature if in their manner and appearance we detect the
qualities that will serve or oppose our purposes. But this is
a wretched attitude, and in this kind of psychology a
peasant, a peddler, or a pettifogging lawyer is superior to
most statesmen and scholars.

[334]

All experience is occult, whereas all unexperienced knowl-
edge is scientific.

[335]

"Clarity" and "truth" are words that we often hear used side
by side, as if they meant more or less the same thing. Yet
they stand for entirely different things! Rarely, very
rarely is the truth clear, and even more rarely is clarity
true! The truth is almost always complex, obscure, and
ambiguous—every statement, especially a "clear" state-
ment, does it violence. "Clarity" is always violence, it is a
violent attempt to simplify what is many-sided, to make
the natural seem understandable or even reasonable.
Clarity is the virtue of maxims. Maxims are charming,
they are useful, educational, witty, informative—but they

are never true. Because the opposite of every maxim is also true.

[336]

A man of reason easily falls in love with systems. He always tends to distrust his instincts.

[337]

A man of reason always feels insecure in the presence of nature and art. Sometimes he looks down on them with contempt, sometimes he overestimates them superstitiously. It's the men of reason who pay millions for works of art or set up reservations for birds, wild animals, and Indians.

[338]

The man of reason believes that he possesses in himself the meaning of the world and of his life. He transfers to the world and to history the appearance of order and purposiveness characteristic of a reasonably ordered life. Consequently, he believes in progress. He sees that men can shoot better and travel faster than formerly, and does not allow himself to see that such steps forward are offset by a thousand steps backward. He believes that modern man is more highly developed than Confucius, Socrates, or Jesus, because modern man has gone further in developing certain technical capacities.

[339]

That good and evil, beautiful and ugly, and all pairs of opposites can be resolved into a unity is an esoteric, secret truth accessible only to the initiate (and often slipping from his grasp as well); it is not an exoteric truth that all can understand and benefit by. It is the wisdom of Lao-tse, who despised virtues and good works. But Lao-tse

95

himself would have been very careful not to offer this
wisdom to the people.

[340]

Time passes and wisdom endures. It changes its forms
and rites but rests at all times on the same foundation: on
the integration of man with the natural order, the cosmic
rhythm. Often, in times of unrest, men may strive for
emancipation from this order, but such pseudo-liberation
leads invariably to slavery. The super-emancipated man
of today is the will-less slave of money and the machine.

[341]

Nothing has been, nothing will be; everything is, every-
thing has essence and presence.

[342]

Knowledge can be communicated, but wisdom cannot. A
man can find it, he can live it, he can be filled and sus-
tained by it, but he cannot utter or teach it. A truth can be
spoken and cloaked in words only if it is one-sided. Every-
thing that can be thought in thoughts and spoken in
words is one-sided. It is lacking in wholeness, roundness,
unity. The world itself, the reality around us and within
us, is never one-sided.

[343]

What is worth saying but can never be wholly said re-
mains eternally one.

[344]

The things we see are the things that are in us. There is
no reality except for the reality we have within us. What
makes the lives of most men so unreal is that they mis-
take the images outside them for reality and never let
their own world speak. It is possible to be happy in this

way. But once a man knows the other way, he is no longer free to go the way of the many.

[345]

This "awakening," so it seemed, had to do not with truth or knowledge, but with reality and the existence and experience of reality. In awakening, we did not penetrate more deeply into the heart of things, into truth; we only grasped, enacted, or suffered the relation of our own self to the momentary situation. We arrived not at laws but at decisions, we attained not to the center of the world, but to the center of our own person. That is why what we experienced was so uncommunicable, so strangely removed from statement and formulation; communications from this realm of life did not seem to number among the purposes of language. If in an exceptional case one of us was understood in some degree, it was by a man in a similar situation, one who shared our suffering or awakening.

[346]

One function of science is to order and simplify the indigestible and make it discernible to the mind. We believe we have discerned certain laws in history and try to take account of them in our view of the historical truth.

And yet, though I have no objection to the student of history approaching it with a touching, childlike faith in the ordering power of the human mind, he ought also and nevertheless to respect the inscrutable truth, reality, and uniqueness of events. The study of history presupposes the knowledge that one is striving for something impossible yet necessary and important. To study history is to plunge into chaos and yet to preserve one's belief in order and meaning.

[347]

A good and authentic truth must allow of being reversed. When something is true, the opposite must also be true. For a truth is only a short formula for a glance at the world from a particular pole, and every pole has its counterpole.

[348]

I am not opposed to investigation and interpretation, but only to the stifling and repression of the naïve by a rational approach.

[349]

Reason in the right place is a good thing, and those who insist on following instinct or intuition in realms of life where reason is a good guide will usually come to grief, and conversely. I only contend that reason must not be granted total claims or equated with the spirit.

[350]

What our reason thinks and says is a flyspeck compared to the life, relationships, and kinships that ebb and flow under the "threshold."

[351]

It is not a matter of words. Every word can just as well mean its contrary. When professors talk, we never notice this. Their words are always so comfortingly unequivocal; they give rise to the illusion that there is such a thing as sure knowledge, communicable in words.

[352]

Intellectual insights are paper.

[353]

Only those who speak of what they have experienced have confidence.

[354]

It is mortally dangerous to submit your intellectual life too one-sidedly to the rule of the instinct-hating spirit, for every fragment of our instinctive life that cannot be fully sublimated causes bitter suffering when we try to repress it.

[355]

All maxims were truths and essential insights in the mind of the man who first uttered them, and yet in the mouth of the first lazy-minded man to parrot them they became absurdities and misunderstandings.

[356]

Wisdom is incommunicable. Wisdom that a wise man tries to communicate always sounds like folly.

[357]

Perhaps after the longing for experience, man's greatest longing is for forgetfulness.

[358]

What is essential to us we experience all alone in ourselves, quite independently of what goes on outside. How the inner rays are projected outward, what myths, dangers, lusts, gods, and devils we make for ourselves, is objectively irrelevant.

[359]

The moment we talk about it, the simplest thing becomes complex and incomprehensible.

[360]

Nature and spirit do not form a harmony, and to the individual who confronts it the world is not a unity; but deep within us there is a yearning for harmony and unity, and the search for them, when undertaken by a man of true greatness and strength, is invariably tragic.

[361]

The pious and the rational genius know each other well, they are drawn to one another by a secret love, and the highest spiritual experience of which we men are capable is a reconciliation between reason and reverence, in which the great opposites recognize each other as equals.

[362]

Soft is stronger than hard, water than rock, love than violence.

[363]

Only those who are themselves in need of being treated kindly can be gentle and forbearing to others.

[364]

I have no defensive weapons against cleverness and highly developed intellectual technique, much less weapons of response and counterattack. But I have a feeling that tells me whether there is a faith behind a man's speeches and writings. With this naïve divining rod I hold my own in my encounters with the philosophers.

[365]

In arguments it is always the optimist who wins.

[366]

Everything is worthy of notice, for everything can be interpreted.

[367]

Confucius, the great systematic philosopher and moralist, Lao-tse's counterpart . . . has been characterized as follows: "Isn't that the man who knows it can't be done but does it just the same?" Nowhere in literature do I find such an example of serenity, humor, and simplicity. I often think of this saying . . . when I consider world events and the utterances of those who are hoping to rule the world in the next years and decades, and to make it perfect. They do like the great Confucius, but behind their doing there is not his knowledge that "it can't be done."

[368]

BOOKS AND READING

Books and Reading

ANYONE WHO HAS MADE himself more or less at home in the immortal world of books will enter into a new relationship not only with the content of a book, but also with the book itself.

Today we meet many young people who regard it as absurd and unworthy of them to love books instead of life itself; life, they think, is much too short and precious; yet they find time to spend several hours six times a week dancing and listening to popular music.

[369]

The purpose of books is not to make dependent people still more dependent, much less to provide those incapable of living with an easy, artificial substitute for life. On the contrary, books have value only if they lead to life and make for a better life; every hour spent reading is a waste of time unless it gives the reader a spark of strength, an intimation of new youth, a breath of fresh air.

[370]

Among tolerably healthy persons, not given to self-doubt, the passionate will love passion in books, the intelligent intelligence, the good goodness; among readers who are not so well balanced, the contrary will often be true: the intensely intellectual will crave for naïve sensuality, the man of uncontrolled passion for controlled coolness.

[371]

Thoughtless, absent reading is very much like walking blindfold through beautiful country. We should read, not in order to forget ourselves and our daily lives, but on the contrary, in order to gain a firmer, more conscious, more mature grip on our own lives. We should come to a book not as a frightened schoolboy to a forbidding teacher or as the town drunkard to a schnapps bottle, but as a mountain climber to the Alps or a soldier to an arsenal, not as fugitives from life.

[372]

Literary history has always struck me as a shadow world, an exploration of dusty archives or crumbling museums. One might even speak of robbing the dead. Sectarians record the opinions of dead sectarians for the benefit of future sectarians. Their controversies have always been battles of sects, far removed from what I regard as the reality of literature. In my opinion we cannot consume literature as a finished dish prepared by others; no, we must master it for ourselves, bit by bit. We ourselves must read the old books and form our own judgments.

True literature will always find readers, for it embodies fundamental human truths and realities. What is dead is dead. In other words, I am able to recognize literary history only as a history of ideas and their social components, only insofar as it explains the social conditions that make a literary epoch understandable.

[373]

The more discernment, sensibility, and alertness to relationships we put into our reading, the more we see every idea and every literary work in its unique individuality and conditionality, and see that all beauty, all charm hinge precisely on this individuality and uniqueness—and nevertheless we seem to see more and more clearly that all these thousands of voices of the peoples strive toward the same goal, invoke the same gods under different names, dream the same dreams, and suffer the same sufferings. In illuminated moments, the reader perceives in the thousandfold fabric of innumerable languages and books, woven through several millennia, a wondrously sublime chimera, the face of man as a unity compounded by magic from a thousand contradictory traits.

[374]

Literature creates a magical space, in which things otherwise incompatible become compatible and the otherwise impossible becomes real. And this imaginary or surreal space has its own counterpart in magical time, the time of poetry, myth, and fairy tale, which contradicts all historical, calendar time and is common to the legends and fairy tales of all peoples . . . Rare as authentic magic may have become, it is still alive in art.

[375]

An old book is always comforting; it speaks to us from a distance, we can listen or not, and when suddenly mighty words flare up, we take them not as we would from a book of today, from an author with such and such a name, but as though at first hand, as we take the cry of a gull or a ray of sunlight.

[376]

We read this or that and struggle for a time through the world of eternal problems, each of which can never be solved but only experienced, and in the end life always throws us back into a situation where we once again attempt the seemingly impossible, where we engage in a seemingly hopeless task with new desire and new zeal. In this age-old game, which seems indeed so hopeless, a thinking man always has this one consolation: that all the states, ideals, epochs of life are not successive and causally connected as in our school systems, but have an eternal, extratemporal existence, so that the kingdom of God and every other human ideal that we project into an astronomically remote future can at any moment become experience and reality.

[377]

To one who knows how to read, reading a book is coming face to face with a strange man's nature and manner of thinking, trying to understand him, and if possible to win him as a friend.

[378]

A good many peasant women, who neither own nor have read any book but the Bible, have found more in it and gained more knowledge, consolation, and joy from it than any spoiled rich man can gain from his priceless library.

[379]

By and large the "individual reader" is less articulate but a lot more intelligent than public opinion, which is molded by a class of insubstantial intellectuals and fortunately is not as powerful as it thinks.

[380]

We often hear it said that to provide the "far-too-many" with the works of the great authors is like casting pearls before swine. That is nonsense. If good literature involves any threat to the naïve mind, the newspapers, which fall into every hand, and even the Bible are at least twice as dangerous.

[381]

In regard to the essence and foundation of all literature, namely, the power of its language, the judgment of the "people" is if anything surer and less easily deceived than that of those who bandy philological and aesthetic analyses and arguments. And especially in the case of negative, disparaging judgments, those coming from the "people" strike me more deeply and painfully than those of the intellectuals.

[382]

I myself incline neither to botany nor to literary criticism. But if I must choose between a cool, sober philological study and an essay overflowing with warmth and enthusiasm, I prefer the former. Science and scholarship are always estimable when they remain on their own ground and do not borrow from other realms of the spirit.

[383]

The "classics" have been selected by the reading public and not by the scholars, who in many respects are far behind the people.

[384]

Generally speaking, the enemies of good books and of good taste are not those who despise books but those who read anything and everything.

[385]

We shall lose nothing by leaving the manuals, surveys, and histories of philosophies unread; any work by an original thinker gives us more, for it compels us to think for ourselves, trains and enhances our consciousness.

[386]

Of all literary pleasures, the reading of a poem is the highest and purest. Only pure lyric poetry can sometimes achieve the perfection, the ideal form wholly permeated by life and feeling, that is otherwise the secret of music.

[387]

The more certain requirements of entertainment and popular education come to be met by other inventions, the more books will regain their dignity and authority. Today we have not quite reached the point where such new inventions as radio, cinema, etc., can relieve the printed book of the functions it can best dispense with.

[388]

Many regard it as a disgrace not to know the latest novel by the latest fashionable author; yet they look down their noses at the "old trash" and do not begin to suspect how much of the latest and most popular literature is old stuff, hastily warmed up and dished out as new.

[389]

Those who have no appreciation of poetry are sure to overlook what is finest and most beautiful in the language of good prose.

[390]

With reading it is the same as with every other pleasure: the more fervently and lovingly we give ourselves to it, the deeper and more lasting the pleasure will be.

[391]

I have often wondered why most of what is written about literature is so strange, so inept and confusing. The reason is that most critics know nothing of the true content of literature. Literature deserving of the name has no other content than the soul, the vibration of the timeless self in the temporal world. But most critics imagine that literature ought, or means, to teach, that it should provide pictures of life, character studies, portraits of professional or social groups, etc. All this is secondary and usually fortuitous. No true writer chooses his material. But his "choice of material" is always criticized. Would anyone think of asking a tenor why he doesn't prefer to sing bass?

[392]

Not two out of a thousand books can arouse the feeling that not the author but things themselves are speaking to us.

[393]

The higher a man's culture (hence his self-knowledge and feeling for his own personality), the more quickly and surely he will reject what is not consonant with his nature, but the more deeply he will absorb everything that is akin to him.

[394]

I know when I lose myself in a beautiful book that I am doing something better, wiser, and more valuable than anything the ministers and kings of this world have done for years. I am building where they destroy, gathering where they disperse, experiencing God, where they deny or crucify Him.

[395]

To kill something that is spiritually alive is harder than to bring something dead back to life.

[396]

Our inner compass is deflected by every book we read; every outside mind shows us from how many other points of view the world can be considered. Then the oscillation gradually dies down, and the needle returns to its old orientation, inherent in the nature of each one of us. This is what happened to me when I stopped reading for a time. One can read so much; a book lover living in seclusion devours books and opinions as a man of the world devours people—one is sometimes amazed at how much one can stand. But then a time comes when one has to throw it all down and walk in the woods for a while, to consult with the weather, the flowers, the mists, and the winds, and find once more within oneself the unchanging standpoint from which one sees the world whole again.

[397]

In my experience one can make no better resolution when on vacation than not to read a line, and nothing is more delightful, when a suitable occasion presents itself, than to break one's resolution with a really good book.

[398]

Everything written fades away sooner or later. The *Weltgeist* reads all books and the fading of all books, and laughs. For us it is a good thing to have read some of them and gained an intimation of their meaning. The meaning that evades all written work, yet dwells in it secretly, is always the same.

[399]

REALITY AND IMAGINATION

Reality and Imagination

T HE ONLY PART of a story that is true is the part the listener believes.

[400]

Just as after leafing through his paper the subscriber enjoys for a moment the illusion that he knows what has been going on in the world for the last twenty-four hours and that nothing of any importance has happened that was not predicted by clever editorialists in the Sunday supplement, so each of us, each day and hour, misrepresents a mysterious jungle as a lovely garden or as a flat, easily intelligible map, the moralist with the help of his maxims, the religious man with the help of his faith, the engineer with his slide rule, the painter with his palette, and the poet with the help of his models and ideals.

[401]

The eye of the will is impure and makes for distortion. Only when we want nothing, only when our gaze becomes pure contemplation, does the soul of things—beauty— open to us. When I look at a forest that I want to buy or cut down or mortgage, I see not the forest but its relation to my will. But when I want nothing of it, when I only look "thoughtlessly" into its green depths, then and then alone is it a forest, is it nature and growth; then and then alone is it beautiful.

[402]

It is an old experience that as though by enchantment we always encounter outside us the problems that concern us inwardly. With striking frequency, a man who is thinking about building a house, getting divorced, or having an operation falls in with men possessed by the same problem. I have had the experience with my reading; at times when I am deeply preoccupied by some life problem, books in which the same problem figures come to me unsought from all sides.

[403]

Boredom is something unknown to nature; it is an invention of city-dwellers.

[404]

When dealing with the insane, the best method is to pretend to be sane.

[405]

No man should look at the world solely with a view to what at the moment or on close scrutiny may prove valuable and important; the pure art of enjoyment, of calm contemplation and acceptance, is a treasure, and no intellectual, however subtle and self-assured, has the right to rob us of it, for if he does he is destroying more culture than all the intelligence in the world can restore.

[406]

Beauty rejoices, not those who possess it, but those who are capable of loving it and worshipping it.

[407]

Our soul has in it a magic we can trust; it seeks wholeness and strives to compensate for every gap, every deficiency. It strives to make up for every incapacity by heightened achievement in another field, and in the weakest, most sensitive, most luckless of men it plays its tenderest, most fervent, most beautiful music, in order to praise life, to say yes, to glorify God.

[408]

Our actions are not determined by abstract insights or considerations; every step we take in life has its source in the primal ground of our being, in our temperament, our race. Afterwards we cast about for a philosophy that conforms with these unconscious motivations.

[409]

Reasons, it seems to me, are always unclear. Causality is to be found nowhere in life, but only in thought. Men do not act on the basis of "reasons," they merely imagine they do, and in the interests of vanity and virtue they try to convince others that this is so.

[410]

To my way of thinking, every truth is so absolutely bipolar that both poles are of equal value—as long as truth is felt, as long as there is life in our thinking, as long as we are serious.

[411]

I have always observed that not only I myself, but also those enviable persons who are able to give reasons for their actions, are never really moved and guided by these reasons. What impels us to act is that we fall in love with something; I own that I am all in favor of such falling in love.

[412]

It is always a strange moment when friends or acquaintances of ours who were hitherto strangers to each other meet. Rarely are expectations fulfilled, even more rarely do we obtain the consolation of seeing our "personality" confirmed and restored to unity: in such situations our self usually proves to be no more than a fragile tent, a momentary point of intersection, without reality or meaning of its own.

[413]

It seems possible that every man's trajectory, like that of a tossed ball, is predetermined and that when he thinks he is tricking destiny, or forcing its hand, he is actually pursuing a course that was laid down long ago. In any event, "destiny" is in ourselves and not outside us, and this gives the surface, the visible events of life, a certain irrelevance. Often the things that we take hard or even tragically are thereby reduced to mere trifles. And the very people who quail at every semblance of tragedy are destroyed by things to which they have never paid attention.

[414]

Some of us know with our heads or our hearts that it is not a question of progress or romanticism, of forward or backward, but of outside and inside, that what we dread is not railroads and motorcars, not money or reason, but only forgetfulness of God, the flattening of the soul.

[415]

Meditation and spiritual exercises lead in gradual stages to insight. Then the ego proves to be an illusion, ego-consciousness is replaced by all-consciousness, the redeemed soul returns to the All from its wanderings in isolation.

[416]

A profession is always a misfortune, it means limitation and resignation.

[417]

"Neuroses" may be diseases and usually they are. But the neurosis of present-day writers may, in the last analysis, be a sign of good health; that is, the only possible reaction of men possessed of souls to an age that knows only money and quality and has no soul.

[418]

Our true possessions are those we do not see and hardly know of.

[419]

The unity that I revere behind multiplicity is not a tedious, gray, intellectual, theoretical unity. It is life itself, full of play, full of sorrow, full of laughter.

[420]

No self, not even the most naïve, is a unity, it is a highly variegated world, a starry firmament in miniature, a chaos of forms, stages, and states, of inherited characters and possibilities. Yet every individual tries to regard this chaos as a unity and speaks of his self as though it were a simple, firmly and clearly delineated entity. This illusion, which is common to all men (even the highest), seems to be a necessity, a requirement of life.

[421]

The truth has a million faces, but there is only one truth.

[422]

The self-confidence you see in certain people seems to be greater than it is. Brave as they may be when together, confront any one of them with a difficult problem when he is all alone, and you will see a big change.

[423]

Meaning and essence are not somewhere behind things, but in them, in all things.

[424]

The world has often been condemned as evil because someone has slept badly or eaten too much. The world has often been glorified because someone has just kissed a girl.

[425]

Nothing is important, nothing is unimportant; the world is a shadow play, but the images of things in our souls have a profound, uncanny reality.

[426]

Everything hostile vanishes and is transcended the moment we succeed in excluding time from our thoughts.

[427]

Utopias are not meant to be slavishly realized, but to make men regard the difficult things for which we nevertheless yearn as possible, and to strengthen our faith in these possibilities.

[428]

Up to a certain degree of intensity, feelings and fantasies gain in power and beauty; beyond that point they grow flat and dull—then it is time to let other fantasies, other sets of feelings rise up.

[429]

No one dreams of what does not concern him.

[430]

Magic is this: to exchange inside and outside, not under compulsion, not passively . . . but freely, of your own volition. Summon up the past, summon up the future: they are both within you. Up until now you have been the slave of what is inside you. Learn to master it. That is magic.

[431]

The distinction between inside and outside is habitual to our thinking, but not necessary. Our mind is capable of passing beyond the dividing line we have drawn for it. Beyond the pairs of opposites of which the world consists, other, new insights begin.

[432]

The magic of dreams often fails us by day, because when awake even the best of dreamers takes the outside world more seriously than he should. The madman manages better; he appoints himself emperor, his cell is his castle, and everything is wonderfully right.

To transform the outside world by magic without going mad—that is our aim. It's not easy, but on the other hand, there isn't much competition.

[433]

I don't know anything about ghosts, I live in my dreams. Other people likewise live in dreams, but not in their own; that's the difference.

[434]

I have never been interested in ghosts and for that reason have never encountered one, but I am certain that I have only to wish it and they will come in swarms. But I don't believe they are more interesting than other people.

[435]

Man is an onion consisting of a hundred skins, a fabric of many threads. The ancient Asians were well aware of this, and Buddhist Yoga devised a precise technique for dispelling the illusion of the personality. The games of mankind are varied and amusing: for a thousand years India has done its utmost to dispel this illusion and the Occident has been at equal pains to consolidate and intensify it.

[436]

Reality is a lightning flash that quivers imprisoned in every stone. If you do not awaken it, the stone remains a stone, the city a city, beauty beautiful, tedium tedious, all sleeping the dream of things until, driven by your high-tension currents, you flood them with the storm we call "reality."

[437]

It is my misfortune always to contradict myself. Reality always does that, only the spirit and virtue do not. After a hard summer walk, for instance, I can be wholly possessed by the desire for a glass of water and regard water as the most wonderful thing on earth. Fifteen minutes later, when my thirst has been quenched, nothing on earth interests me less than water and drinking. It is the same with eating, sleeping, and thinking. My attitude toward the so-called intellect is exactly the same as toward eating and drinking. Sometimes there is nothing in all the world that attracts me so forcefully and seems to me so indispensable as intellectual life, the possibility of abstraction, of logic, of ideas. But then when I have had my fill of it, when I need and desire the opposite, all thought disgusts me like spoiled food. I know from experience that such an attitude is held to be arbitrary, lacking in character, even inadmissible; but I have never been able to understand why. For just as I cannot help alternating between eating and fasting, sleeping and waking, so I cannot help shuttling back and forth between natural life and intellectualism, between experience and Platonism, order and revolution, Catholicism and the spirit of the Reformation. A man capable of worshipping the intellect and despising nature all his life, of being always a revolutionary and never a conservative, or conversely, would indeed impress me as highly virtuous, steadfast, and full of character, but at the same time such conduct seems to me as fatal, repugnant, and insane as wanting to eat or to sleep all the time. And yet all parties and movements, whether political, intellectual, religious, or scientific, are built on the assumption that such insane conduct is possible and natural.

[438]

The cathedrals that are being destroyed today should not be rebuilt. They are only stone. But their spirit should regain power. Then the stone will be no loss.

[439]

The world outside the lunatic asylums is no less weird than the world inside.

[440]

We run about on this earth, always on the move, and often we wave our hats and cry out greetings just when our fellow wanderer is in the valley below, invisible and perhaps in utter darkness.

[441]

The philosophy of our times describes human life as a being-thrown-into-the-world. This does not satisfy me. It is only a hysterical attempt to disguise inadequacy as tragedy. When this is done, the lofty concept of "tragedy" loses all value and merely because he was born and is unable to make anything of himself man becomes a kind of hero.

[442]

Tragedies can never be prevented, for they are not accidents but clashes between opposing worlds.

[443]

Like all boys, I loved and envied certain callings: the hunter, the raftsman, the carter, the tightrope walker, the arctic explorer. But far more than anything else I would like to have become a magician. That was my deepest, most fervent drive—a certain dissatisfaction with what people called reality, which struck me at times as nothing more than an absurd conspiracy on the part of grownups; at an early age, sometimes in fear and sometimes in scorn, I rejected this reality and burned with desire to enchant it; to transform it, to transcend it.

[444]

I think a lot more of a man who is prepared to give himself heart and soul to the naïvest ideals in the world than of one who can talk intelligently about causes and ideals but is incapable of making the slightest sacrifice to any.

[445]

Sentimentality is a basking in feelings that in reality you don't take seriously enough to make the slightest sacrifice to or ever translate into action.

[446]

There is no sentimentality in nature.

[447]

A time will come when the notion of relativity will be extended to the realm of sickness and health; today's sicknesses will be tomorrow's health, and it will be recognized that never being sick for a day is not always the most reliable symptom of health.

[448]

What a lesser man sees in a greater is just so much as he is capable of seeing.

[449]

Our instincts have an amazing gift of disguising themselves as a *Weltanschauung*.

[450]

It is difficult not to overestimate the virtues we have. It is even more difficult not to overestimate the virtues we should like to have. It is easy to underestimate the sufferings of others. It is even easier to overestimate the happiness of others.

[451]

One night when I had to help a woman in labor, I saw that the greatest pain and the greatest ecstasy have a very similar expression.

[452]

We are uneasy only as long as we have hope.

[453]

Half the romance of travel consists in the expectation of adventure. The other half is an unconscious impulse to transform and disperse our erotic drive. We wanderers have a way of cherishing dreams of love precisely because we know they cannot come true, and of playfully distributing the love that belongs by right to a woman among villages and mountains, lakes and chasms, children by the wayside, the beggar on the bridge, cows at pasture, birds and butterflies. We detach love from its object, we are satisfied with love itself, just as in wandering we have no destination in mind but only the pleasure of wandering itself, of being on the move.

[454]

The poetry of travel lies in the organic integration of new experience, in the growth of our understanding for unity in diversity, in a new encounter, under new conditions, with old truths and old laws.

[455]

What makes strange lands so strange is not that we are surrounded by new and unfamiliar things and people, but that we ourselves are strangers wherever we go, that we arouse laughter or astonishment and are not accepted and befriended by others as a matter of course.

[456]

It is not until some time after we have left it that a place where we have stayed for a while takes form in our memory and becomes an unchanging image. As long as we are there and able to see it all, we perceive essentials and incidentals with just about equal intensity. Later on, our secondary impressions fade and our memory retains only what is worth retaining; if this were not so, how could we look back over so much as a single year of our life without a sickening, terrifying confusion?

[457]

The world, I am told, has seen many men who had a good deal of the dog or the fox, the fish or the snake about them, yet incurred no special difficulties on that account. Quite a few who have made impressive careers have owed their success more to the fox or the ape in them than to anything human.

[458]

ART AND THE ARTIST

Art and the Artist

ART IS A COMBINATION of the paternal and maternal world, of spirit and blood; it can begin with sensation and lead to extreme abstraction, or begin in a pure world of ideas and end in quivering flesh. All works of art that are not mere sleight of hand have this dangerously smiling double face, this male-female quality, this mixture of instinct and pure spirit.

[459]

Nature has ten thousand colors, and we have taken it into our heads to reduce the scale to twenty.

[460]

Only the symbol endures, not the copy.

[461]

The beginning of all art is love. The value and scope of all art are determined by the artist's capacity for love.

[462]

Nothing is as joyful, and nothing can give so much joy, as beauty and art—that is, if our immersion in beauty and art is so complete that we forget ourselves and the burning pain of the world. It need not be a Bach fugue or a painting by Giorgione; a patch of blue in a cloudy sky, the nimble fan of a seagull's tail, the rainbow colors in a spot of oil—these and far less suffice.

When we return from such happiness to self-awareness and to our knowledge of life's misery, our joy returns to sadness, the world shows us not its radiant sky but the blackness underneath, and then beauty and art make us sad. But they remain beautiful, they remain divine, and this is true of the fugue, the painting, the gull's tail feathers, the oil spot, and of far lesser things.

And even though the joy of forgetting oneself and the world lasts only for brief moments, the sorrow-steeped enchantment that rises from the miracle of beauty can endure for hours, for a lifetime.

[463]

Preoccupation with irrational, strange, uncanny forms in nature gives us a feeling that a kinship exists between our innermost being and the will that created such forms. Soon we are tempted to regard them as our own moods, our own creations; we see the boundaries between ourselves and nature waver and melt away and can no longer tell whether the images on our retina spring from outward or from inner impressions. An experience of this kind is the simplest means of discovering how creative we are, how deeply our soul participates in the perpetual creation of the world. The same indivisible divinity is indeed at work in us and in nature, and if the outside world were to perish, one of us would be capable of rebuilding it, for mountain and stream, leaf and tree, root and flower, everything that has ever been formed in nature lies preformed within us, springs from the soul whose essence is eternity. This essence is beyond our knowledge; but, primarily as the power to love and to create, it reveals itself to our feeling.

[464]

All our art is merely compensation, a painstaking compensation far too dearly bought, for lost life, lost animal-

ity, lost love. And yet again this is not so. To regard
spiritual life as a mere substitute for a deficient life of the
senses is to overestimate the senses. The life of the senses
is not worth a jot more than the life of the spirit, or
conversely. To embrace a woman or to write a poem
amounts to the same thing.

[465]

At certain moments we are capable of insight into the
secret of unity; but our capacity for love depends on our
ability to evaluate, to evaluate subjectively; without it
there can be neither art nor love.

[466]

Art is the contemplation of the world in a state of grace.

[467]

Just as every great work of art springs from love, so the
only worthy and helpful approach to works of art is love.

[468]

I know that today just as at any time in the past every
true poem or painting, every measure of true music is
paid for with life, with suffering and blood. Nothing has
changed in the world except for what has always been on
the surface and readily changeable: public opinion and
conventional morality. Fortunately any serious artist can
defend himself against these: it takes a bit of asceticism
and renunciation, but is very much worthwhile.

[469]

Insofar as culture is merely a matter of fashion and a
form of life for the masses, it is possible to make predic-
tions about it, but insofar as it is creation and spirit, it is
produced by a very small minority and fits into no causal

system. It will seem to only when future generations look back at it.

[470]

Art has to do with condensations, with images. You people want concepts instead of images.

[471]

Whether art and beauty can really make man better and stronger is an open question; but one thing is certain: that like the starry firmament they remind us of light, of order and harmony, and of "meaning" amid chaos.

[472]

Genius is the power of love, a yearning for devotion.

[473]

Serenity is the virtue of saints and knights; it is the secret of the beautiful and the very substance of all art. The poet who praises the grandeur and dread of life in the dance step of his verses, the musician who makes them resound as pure presence, is a bringer of light, a bestower of joy and brightness on earth, even if he must first lead us through tears and painful conflict.

[474]

Such gaiety implies neither trifling nor complacency; it is supreme insight and love, an affirmation of all reality, waking consciousness at the brink of the depths. It is the secret of beauty and the very substance of all art.

[475]

Art reveals new faces, new languages, new gestures and stammerings; it is sick of speaking the language of yesterday and the day before, it wants to dance, to kick over the traces, to tilt its hat, to reel and zigzag. And our fellow citizens are furious, they feel they are being mocked, that the very root, the intrinsic value of their existence is being held up to doubt; they hurl invective and pull the blanket of their culture over their ears. The selfsame citizen whom the slightest offense to his personal dignity sends running to the judge has become a mine of bloodcurdling insults.

[476]

We make our music, and sometimes, through a misunderstanding, someone throws a penny in our hat, because he thinks our music is didactic or moral or otherwise clever. If he knew it was nothing but music he would pass on and keep his penny.

[477]

I would not want to live for the sake of life alone; I would not want to love for the woman's sake alone. I need the detour of art; if I am to be satisfied with life, if I am to bear it, I need the lonely, intricate pleasure of being an artist.

[478]

The understanding of art and the ability to experience it require a natural predisposition, which must be related to the artistic drive, or talent. Those who have it are capable of artistic pleasures; others are not.

[479]

Arguments about art are like all arguments about opinions. Men cannot understand one another unless they love one another. They can love one another only if they experience the world more in themselves than outside themselves.

[480]

Talent must be opposed and counterbalanced by character, inspiration by discipline, facility by inhibitions.

[481]

It must be permissible to recall now and then that in its great poets a people possesses not merely a variety of high-class jesters and entertainers, in whose company one can occasionally spend a few pleasant hours, but something essentially different, namely, antennae, sensitive feelers, which as it were anticipate and test a segment of the future, a possibility of development. Poets and thinkers, insofar as they were not timeservers but had the courage of their own convictions, are a people's noblest but also most dangerous models. For these models do not provide a standard list of duties and convictions that need only be imitated, but show and teach the exact opposite, namely, the way to solitude and personal conscience.

[482]

What our times need and cry out for is not adroit, bustling bureaucrats but personality, conscience, and responsibility. Intellect and "talent" are in oversupply.

[483]

Even the most insignificant work of art, a pencil sketch consisting of six lines, or a four-line poem, aims boldly and blindly at the impossible; it is a striving for totality, an attempt to enclose chaos in a nutshell!

[484]

The men who have striven to rise from time to the timeless have never been vague dreamers, but have always had deep roots of responsibility in their own times. The more we learn about them, the more symbolic and hence exemplary they become.

[485]

If industry and science no longer need personalities, let them do without. But now as much as ever we artists, who amid the general bankruptcy of culture inhabit an island that still offers tolerable possibilities of life, must obey other laws. For us personality is not a luxury but an indispensable condition of existence; it is the joy of life, an inalienable capital. And by artists I mean all those to whom it is a necessity to feel that they are alive and growing, to be conscious of the foundations of their powers, and on these foundations to build their lives in accordance with inborn laws, in other words, to avoid all irrelevant activities and steps in life that do not stand in the same meaningful relation to the foundation as vault to wall or roof to pillar in a good piece of architecture.

[486]

In art it is the timeless, not the timely, that matters.

[487]

All true talent is rooted in sensibility, in a well-endowed body and senses.

[488]

With a slight exaggeration we artists might say: The value of my work is measured by the pleasure it gave me to do it. What endures and remains lastingly effective is not what has been willed, thought out, constructed, but the gesture, the moment's inspiration, the ephemeral magic. Just as the value of a Mozart opera resides not in the plot or moral but in the gesture and melody, in the freshness and charm with which a number of musical themes flow and change.

[489]

The powers of enjoyment and of memory are interdependent. To enjoy is to squeeze every last drop of sweetness out of a fruit. And to remember is the art not only of holding fast to what has once been enjoyed, but of molding it to ever purer form.

[490]

And something else that I'm old-fashioned about: I don't reject or hate feeling and sentimentality. Instead, I ask: How do we live, how do we know we are alive, except by our feelings? What good to me is a full pocketbook, a thriving bank account, a natty crease in my trousers, or a pretty girl if they inspire no feeling, if my soul is unmoved? No, I am capable of hating sentimentalities in others, but in myself I love them and tend to coddle them. Feelings, sensitive, easily stirred emotional vibrations— these, I must own, are my heritage, all I have to see me through life. If I were dependent on my muscular strength and had become a wrestler or boxer, no one would expect me to look down on muscular strength. If I were an expert at mental arithmetic and had become chief clerk in a large office, no one would expect me to despise mental arithmetic. But a poet is expected—and some young poets demand it of themselves—to hate and feel ashamed of the very qualities that make the poet, emotional resilience, the ability to fall in love, to burn with enthusiasm, to give himself, and to attain new heights of experience in the world of feeling; they expect him to reject and resist anything that might be termed "sentimental." Well, let them do as they like, I can't go along, to me my feelings are a thousand times more precious than all the aggressiveness of the world, and during the war years they preserved me from participating in aggressive sentimentality.

[491]

Yes, we lack business sense and spirit of enterprise; and this lack has its counterpart among our antipodes, the enterprising businessmen, in a deficient psychic dimension. Our romantic-poetic infantilism is no more infantile than the childlike pride and confidence of the world-conquering engineer, who believes in his slide rule as we believe in our God, and who flies into a paroxysm of rage or fear when the absolute certainty of the rules governing his world is shaken by Einstein. We romantics and sentimentalists—for that is what the big-city literati most often call us—are not all of us stupid fanatics, who rush into print and mobilize the home guards whenever an old building is condemned; some of us are almost as intelligent as certain members of the profit-and-efficiency party. At heart perhaps we have more faith in the future, and look forward to it more eagerly, than many of those who make a cult of progress.

[492]

I regard the loneliness of the artist, and of gifted men in general, as inevitable, regardless of whether they are successful or not. I find it just as understandable, and fundamentally right, that a gifted man, a man of imagination, should conceal this loneliness as much as possible. For though sooner or later the man of talent is bound to notice the dreary limitations of the average man, he must guard against this insight because in the end it would lead to a lovelessness, a contempt for mankind, which he himself would be unable to bear. But concealed or not, the great, often icy loneliness of the artist or thinker in the midst of average men is always with us; it is the price we have to pay for having a certain advantage over others.

[493]

No one is more vain, more intent on echo and approval than the thinker, and indeed he is bitterly in need of echo and approval.

[494]

The bourgeois often likens the imaginative man to a madman. He rightly suspects that he himself would go mad if he were to confront his own depths as an artist, religious man, or philosopher does. Regardless of whether we call these depths the soul or the unconscious or something else, they are the source of every one of our life impulses. Between himself and his soul the bourgeois has appointed a policeman, a consciousness, a morality, a border authority, and he recognizes nothing that comes from the depths of the soul unless it is first stamped by that authority. The artist, on the other hand, must eternally distrust not the land of the soul, but all border authorities; he passes secretly between Here and There, between Conscious and Unconscious as though he were at home on both sides.

[495]

In our modern bourgeois world, which today to be sure is trembling in its foundations, the artist is a kind of surrogate figure, to whom the bourgeoisie entrust functions which should properly be the concern of every man, but which in these decadent times are neglected by most of the bourgeoisie. Today artists are the only class of men able to live, unmolested and very largely tolerated by society, in accordance with their own natures. This allows them to fulfill a commandment that is graven on the hearts of all men, but which in most is stifled by the dreary struggle for day-to-day existence.

[496]

Wherever genius makes its appearance, it is either stifled by its environment, or tyrannizes it; it is universally regarded as the finest flower of mankind, yet everywhere creates trouble and confusion. It always appears singly, is condemned to loneliness, is incorruptible, and always has a tendency to self-sacrifice.

[497]

I regard genius in all its forms as an attempt on the part of nature to provide, at the cost of great sacrifice, an exemplar of a better, more successful, more viable type of man.

[498]

We see that no civilization is possible without violence to nature, that civilized man is gradually transforming the whole earth into a tedious, bloodless landscape of concrete and sheet metal, that every impulse, however virtuous and idealistic, leads invariably to violence, war, and sorrow, that the average man would be unable to endure life without the help of genius, yet is the sworn enemy of genius and always will be.

[499]

When I speak of genius as a biological problem, I mean that genius, as exemplified in truly outstanding men, almost always has a tragic life and lives in the bleak light of approaching doom. This has nothing in common with the philistine bourgeois theory that genius is always related to madness. No, if genius, life raised to its highest intensity, swings so often to its counterpole, to death or madness, it is because in genius human existence recognizes itself as a terrible misfortune, a great and daring but not entirely successful project of nature. Universally recognized as the noblest and most desirable fruit on the tree of mankind, genius is in no wise protected, much less reproduced, by biological mechanisms; it is a beacon and goal of yearning to the life it is born into, but in that life it cannot but stifle.

[500]

The artist's one advantage is this: that his lunacy is not locked up but enjoys a certain standing because of its products.

[501]

All higher individuation turns against the ego and tends to destroy it.

[502]

From the careers of so-called geniuses we tend to draw the comforting inference that every really strong and gifted man has found his way and created the works that were in him. This is a cowardly consolation and a lie; in reality, many of these famous men, despite high achievement, were unable to fulfill their talents and vocation; in all periods of history, moreover, any number of gifted men have failed to achieve goals worthy of them, and many careers have been broken and ground into misery.

[503]

I see the world as an artist; though I believe I am a democrat in my thinking, in my feeling I am an aristocrat, that is, I am able to love quality of all kinds, but not quantity.

[504]

Art should not be subject to constraint of any kind. The art lover who is not happy about contemporary art should neither condemn it, nor force himself to "enjoy" it. Since in music, for example, we possess and succeed in enjoying the works of almost three centuries, we should not demand that the composers of today abandon their experiments and innovations, which after all make the world of music not poorer but richer. If modern music sometimes strikes us as cold and constructed, we should bear in mind that it is a reaction to more than half a century of music that may well be excessively sweet and sensuous.

[505]

The mystic tries to annul time by contemplative renunciation of all action. The artist strives to do the same thing in the opposite way: by preserving and perpetuating through heightened activity.

[506]

Down through the centuries there have been hundreds of "ideologies" and parties, programs and revolutions; they have changed the world and (possibly) brought progress. But none of their programs or declarations of principles has survived its time. The paintings and words of a few great artists, the words of a few authentic wise men and lovers and creators have survived their times. Centuries after they were spoken, the words of Jesus or of an ancient poet have stirred innumerable men, awakened them, opened their eyes to the sufferings and wonders of mankind. It is my hope and ambition to figure in the ranks of these lovers and witnesses, to be one among thousands, not to be regarded as a "genius" or anything like that.

[507]

What is new and interesting today ceases to be so tomorrow. But those things that have survived several centuries and not yet been forgotten or destroyed—it seems unlikely that their repute will fluctuate very appreciably in our lifetime.

[508]

In theologians and others, the intellect is always rather too much inclined to concepts, to leveling, to classifica-

tion. It contents itself with "tree," whereas body and soul
have no use for "tree," but need and love linden, oak, and
maple. That is why I believe artists are nearer to God's
heart than thinkers. If God expresses Himself differently
in an Indian or Chinese than in a Greek, it is not a failing,
it is superabundant wealth. If we try to subsume all these
manifestations of the divine under one concept, we shall
have no oaks and maples, but at best "trees."

[509]

Spirit and soul, intellect and feeling are inseparable and
interdependent; anyone who overestimates and overculti-
vates one at the expense of the other, or worse, in conflict
with the other, is aiming at the half rather than the
whole.

It is amusing to note that the pure intellectual, for all
the aptness and acuteness of his judgments, soon grows
tiresome. And the lofty enthusiasts of feeling, the poetic
specialists of the heart soon grow equally tiresome. A
noble intellect that relies on itself alone and feeling re-
duced to its own resources both lack a dimension. We see
this in daily life and in politics; in art it is still more
evident.

[510]

If I have all the works of Bach and Haydn in my head and
am able to say the cleverest things about them, it does no
one a particle of good. But if I pick up my tin whistle and
play a lively shimmy, the shimmy may be good or bad, but
in either case it gives people pleasure; it goes to their legs
and blood. That's what counts.

[511]

"Interpretation" is a game of the intellect, often a very
amusing game, good for clever people with no feeling for

art, who are able to write books about Negro sculpture or diatonic music, but never penetrate to the core of a work of art, because they stand at the gate, trying their luck with a hundred keys, failing to see that the gate is open.

[512]

It is always a mistake to talk about the "function" of art, about what art or the artist "should" do; no good ever comes of it. The artist has no "should"; a true artist is not moved by any sense of obligation, but by instinct; he simply does what his nature bids him . . . But in a very different and wider sense the artist, like every man of above-average powers and sensibilities, has his importance for the future of mankind. Every one of these original, sensitive, passionate, and restless men is an attempt on the part of mankind to unfold and attain new possibilities, and the more the author senses this and expresses it in his works, the greater will be their effect, though perhaps not at the moment.

[513]

The dilettante is inferior to the specialist in ability, in his command of means and methods, but he is superior in the freedom and candor with which he does what gives him pleasure and expresses what is important to him, without the specialist's scruples, ambitions, and inhibitions.

[514]

The born dilettantes, who seem to make up so large a part of mankind, might be described as caricatures of free will. Far removed from nature and from the knowledge of necessity, they lack the ability innate in every original artist to perceive the call of nature within them. Thus they drift along frivolously and irresolutely, leading worthless and apparently aimless lives. Since they have nothing of their own inside them, they can only imitate; apes of nature, they make an irresponsible game of doing what they see others doing out of inner drive and necessity.

[515]

The highest art has no need of explanation or applied psychology; it sets down its creations and trusts in their magic, without fear of not being understood.

[516]

To the creative artist space, time, causality, and the content of sense perception are essential realities; he cannot doubt them, for they are his only means of representing anything convincingly.

[517]

It makes no difference what subject a writer "chooses." It makes no difference, because such "choosing" does not take place; it is merely an invention of the professors who write histories of literature.

[518]

Your belief that the function of literature is to provide the people with simple, wholesome, pleasing fare that will help them to avoid conflicts is undoubtedly shared by Herr Goebbels and General Franco. Various opinions are possible about the kind of art that should be produced, but unfortunately the whole question concerns only the manufacturers of art and not true artists, for true artists have no choice about what they are going to do.

[519]

As long as there is life on earth, men will not cease to tell each other what they have experienced and communicate that part of their experience which has remained an inner possession. And among these men there will always be some whose experience becomes for them an expression and symbol of age-old cosmic laws, who in the perishable perceive the eternal and in the changing and contingent the imprint of the divine. It will not matter very much whether such writers call their works novels, memoirs, confessions, or something else.

[520]

Never has a human language (I mean a verbal one) achieved half the rhythm and wit, the radiance and spirit that a cat expends in the windings of its tail, a bird of paradise in the silvery glitter of its wedding dress. Nevertheless, whenever man has been himself instead of trying to imitate the ants or bees, he has outdone the bird of paradise, the cat, and all other plants and animals. He has devised languages that communicate meaning and vibration far better than German, Greek, or Italian. He has conjured up religions, buildings, paintings, and philosophies, he has created music that far exceeds any bird of paradise in play of expression and richness of color.

[521]

There is no such thing as good, authentic language as an end in itself; language is good and authentic when it is an expression of authentic experience. That is why the language of the people, full of age-old suprapersonal experience, is always so beautiful. If the average German of today has so poor a command of his own language, no lack of schooling is to blame, but a flaw in his innermost being, an incapacity for authentic, intense experience.

[522]

A piece of literature is not only content; the more its artistic alchemy transforms content into form, line, and melody, the more worthy it is to be called literature.

[523]

Because I believe in pure categories, I regard it as utterly mistaken to look for ideologies in literature, or for enlightenment in fields that are much better dealt with in non-literary works.

[524]

Literature does not serve purposes, except unconsciously in the sense that all our living powers serve one another. The more didactic literature is, the more it concentrates on the teachings it is trying to impart, the more unsuccessful it is as literature.

[525]

An intense poetic picture of psychic processes, even if it cannot interpret them fully, is more effective and more moving than any purely intellectual analysis.

[526]

Between the world of machines and the world of intellectual bustle, the poet, the purest type of spiritual man, has been driven into a kind of vacuum where he is condemned to suffocate. For the poet is the champion and advocate of precisely those human powers and needs on which our times have fanatically declared war.

[527]

The function of the poet is not to point out ways, but most of all to arouse longing.

[528]

A writer should love not his public but mankind, the better part of which do not read his books, but need them nonetheless.

[529]

Whether a writer produces an effect does not depend on any particular faculty, on technique, intelligence, or taste, but on the distinction of his nature, on the vigor and fullness with which he expresses his type.

[530]

When a writer receives praise or blame, when he arouses sympathy or is ridiculed, when he is loved or rejected, it is not on the strength of his thoughts and dreams as a whole, but only of that infinitesimal part which has been able to make its way through the narrow channel of language and the equally narrow channel of the reader's understanding.

[531]

An author's work stands in the same relationship to what he wanted to say as your attempt to write down your dream stands to the world encompassed in your dream.

[532]

What every true work strives for, regardless of its technique, is harmony, if only between the author's experience and his means of expressing it. Where such harmony is achieved and a sketch or note becomes a literary work that sees and interprets a segment of life as a coherent whole, then we smile and nod gratefully. We bother our heads very little about the technique and temporal garb and are merely glad that another good thing has come into the world.

[533]

Luckily the fame and survival of outstanding works of literature have never depended on learned opinions, and thank the Lord that good, viable works have always made their own way, whereas even the most zealous attempts to galvanize dead glories have seldom or never been successful.

[534]

Tradition is a strange thing, a mystery, almost a sacrament. We become acquainted with a tradition; for a time we associate names, trends, and programs with it; but then little by little, over the years and decades, we see that behind all these names and trends, which we may have rejected long since, there lies a mystery, a nameless heritage, which reaches back not only to the Romantics or to Goethe, to the Middle Ages or antiquity, but to the oldest mythologies, the ideas of primitive peoples, and is wide enough to encompass the most divergent of men and the most contradictory programs, but excludes only one thing: the striving for novelty at all costs.

[535]

Books require neither explanation nor vindication; they are very patient and quite able to wait. If they are any good, they tend to live a good deal longer than the people who argue about them.

[536]

Abstract thinking is a danger to a writer; indeed, it is the greatest of dangers, for if pursued consistently it negates and kills artistic creation.

[537]

There may be collectivist ideas and sermons, but there is no such thing as collectivist literature.

[538]

The future is never born of those who close their eyes to the despair of others. One of the writer's functions is to disclose the hidden depths and make men aware of them.

[539]

Any attempt to go "back to nature" is hopeless and can only come to grief.

[540]

Personality can arise only through the sublimation of animal instincts. For this reason, if for no other, coprophilia in literature would seem to have no future.

[541]

Cognition and creation, to be a thinker and to be an artist are mutually exclusive contraries. It is a mistake to suppose that thinking and creative writing are roughly the same thing and that it is the function of literature to expound philosophies.

[542]

The belief that literature, including poetry, should not be an instrument in the struggles of the moment but should strive for a spirituality above the parties cannot so easily be disposed of as chimerical. A few (admittedly very few) of the more gifted authors are well aware of the situation and do not shirk the duty of analyzing it; these few men live in an isolation that is becoming more oppressive from year to year, and their attempts to give expression to this spiritual crisis are not summer reading but responsible statements. The socialist future will not find its best heralds in the authors who rush head over heels to join the party after the first victory of the coming revolution.

[543]

During the war, artists, poets, and intellectuals were turned into soldiers and ditch diggers. Now an attempt is being made to "politicize" them and make them into organs of political development. One might as well drive nails with a barometer.

[544]

A man of letters should believe in the light; he should be wide open to the light and learn to know it through incontrovertible experience. But he should not regard himself as a bringer of light, much less as a light. If he does, the window will close and the light, which is far from being dependent on us, will go other ways.

[545]

When someone asks the author of an authentic work, "Wouldn't you rather have chosen a different subject?"— it is as if a doctor were to say to a pneumonia patient, "Oh, if only you had decided to have a cold instead!"

[546]

When a man wants to portray himself, it ultimately amounts to the same thing whether he expounds a philosophy of life or tells an anecdote.

[547]

In thinking as in writing, what matters is not the What, not the more or less fortuitous objects of thought, but the intensity, the degree of warmth and purity, with which an individual experiences and thinks out the problems of his day.

[548]

I am not at all of the opinion that an honest author is free to choose his "subject matter." On the contrary, I hold that subjects come to us, not we to them, so that our apparent "choice" is not the act of an arbitrary personal will but, like every decision, the product of an unbroken determinism. On the other hand, I should not like to give the impression that I regard every idea that enters an author's head and every work he produces as justified. On the contrary, I gladly own and am fully convinced that here, as in every other province of life, determinism by no means precludes personal responsibility. Conscience provides us with an unerring standard. Consequently literary conscience is the only law that a writer must under all circumstances obey and cannot evade without injury to himself and his work.

[549]

You assume that a writer's skill in formulation liberates him from the burden of his experience. Something of the kind does indeed take place; there can be a certain liberation in merely getting things off one's chest. But this requires no artistry; the simplest confession or communication to a friend performs the same function as the best poem. The situation of the artist is very different. True, in expressing an experience he partly (never completely) raises it to consciousness, but far from dissipating the experience in his mind, this usually serves only to intensify it.

[550]

An artist always tends to put his whole being into his confession, to identify his whole mission and achievement with it, and consequently to go round and round in the magic circle of his own personal affairs. For an artist always has to exaggerate the importance of his work, because he has transferred the entire content of his existence, and hence his self-justification, from his life to his work.

[551]

It is possible to be a writer, but not to become one.

[552]

If sound opinions and good will were enough, the world would be full of outstanding writers.

[553]

Originality at the expense of intelligibility and clear, transparent form is not art.

[554]

There is far more pleasure in writing bad poems than in reading the best.

[555]

No one writes so badly as the proponents of aging ideologies.

[556]

You are wrong if you think it impossible to "write away a sorrow." Often a good deal of the poison sticks to the verses. In any case, they liquefy the pain. It drains most obligingly from the bumpiest trochees.

[557]

It is a delusion to suppose that poetry can spring from "feeling alone"; it cannot. Form, language, prosody, and choice of words are needed, and these are supplied not by "feeling" but by thought. True, many lesser poets choose their forms unconsciously; that is, they imitate verse forms from memory, but it makes no difference that they do not know what they are doing. None of the masters, from Pindar to Rilke, wrote "by feeling alone" as you put it; every line required rigorous selection and hard work, intense concentration, and often the most painstaking study of the traditional laws and forms. In a pinch letters or editorials can be written "by feeling"; not poetry.

[558]

The reason why a poet cannot live by his work, whereas thousands of journalists seem to be able to, is that ninety percent of what people spend for their cultural needs is spent on newspapers. Consequently, the newspapers provide many with an excellent meal ticket. I am sure many of these journalists are honest workers and men of good will; but it never dawns on them that they and their newspapers are the wall that separates the people from culture.

[559]

The lyric poet, as I observe in others and know by my own experience, does something else besides expressing his thoughts and feelings to the best of his abilities. While he is doing just this, something comes to him from language itself, from its inherent mythical and magical, tonal and rhythmic, pictorial and evocative powers, something that did not originate with him but helps him and often at the same time lures him away from his explicit designs. For language, his instrument, is not merely a dead instrument but also a creative force, less rational but far more powerful than the poet himself. Often when he puts down a word in the belief that he is only expressing something limited and subjective, this same word sends out a stream of acoustic, visual, and emotional associations, which carries him in a direction different from what the helmsman intended. Thus what comes into being in a poem and distinguishes it from a rational text is something unique and never to be repeated, something that is never quite identical with what the author originally intended. What we consciously or unconsciously love in a poem is just this.

[560]

It is easy to delineate the complicated characters of intellectuals, because these can be analyzed and dissected; but only a great artist can portray the simple, organic, and naïvely primitive.

[561]

As far as I can recall, I have always held that the function of the writer is to remember, not to forget, to preserve the transient in words, to conjure up the past by evocation and loving portrayal. True, a trace of the old idealist tradition of the writer as teacher or prophet and preacher has clung to me. But I have always taken this less in the sense of instruction and edification than in the sense of a summons to instill soul and spirit into life.

[562]

The situation of a writer today is similar to that of a Protestant minister; he stands in an empty church and preaches. When people enter the church, when they sit down and listen, he is almost terror-stricken, because he is no longer used to it. But of course he is pleased.

[563]

All my work is a product of weakness, of suffering, not of joyful exuberance, as laymen sometimes suppose of a writer.

[564]

Clever talk about art and literature has become a mockery and an end in itself, and the striving to understand them through critical analysis has done untold harm to the elementary ability to see, hear, and be carried away. If you are content to squeeze the ideas, the message, the educational content out of a poem or story, you are content with very little; the secret, the authentic truth of art will be lost to you.

[565]

It is possible to be a thinker and yet to write well. But it is still customary in Germany to classify a thinker who writes well as a writer—probably because, though most of our writers are not thinkers, they write the kind of German for which ordinarily only thinkers are forgiven.

[566]

We all know that every author of a successful book is a genius, but only up to the hundredth printing. Once this limit is passed, the genius becomes an idiot in the eyes of the critic.

[567]

What the world wants of a writer is not works and thoughts, but his address and personality, so as to honor him, then throw him out, to dress him in finery, then strip him bare, to enjoy him, and then spit at him.

[568]

People have an odd way of claiming their rights to a name that has become known, be it the name of a child prodigy, of a composer, poet, or murderer. One wants his picture, another a sample of his handwriting, the third begs for money; a young colleague sends his manuscript, asking for an opinion, and if the celebrity fails to answer or gives his honest opinion the same admirer grows angry, vengeful, and insulting. The magazines want to print the famous man's picture, the newspapers carry stories about his life, genealogy, and appearance. Old school friends call his attention to their existence and distant relatives claim to have said years before that their cousin would one day be famous.

[569]

For the beneficiary . . . prizes and honors are neither a pleasure nor a festive occasion, nor a merited reward. They are a small component of the complex phenomenon—resulting largely from misunderstandings—that is known as fame, and should be accepted for what they are: attempts on the part of the official world to overcome its embarrassment in the presence of unofficial achievement. On both sides they are a symbolic gesture, an expression of good breeding and courtesy.

[570]

Just as a Nobel Prize can fall on one's head, so can a flowerpot; to tell the truth, the latter happens more frequently.

[571]

Fame and birthday celebrations are an attempt to express spiritual functions in sociological terms or to find a common denominator between spiritual achievement and mass, or quantity.

[572]

All unusually gifted young men with more talent than character are in danger of succumbing to bohemianism. Tempting as it may be, bohemianism today is regressive, a misguided form of life that has become inherently impossible. The artist who persists in it is not a genius or a revolutionary, but simply a poor devil, neither intelligent nor strong enough to work out a valid life of his own.

[573]

Acrobats have one advantage over so-called artists: they have to know what they are doing; otherwise, they break their necks.

[574]

Caricatures have to be excellent; there is no justification for poor ones.

[575]

It is impossible to keep doing the same thing without going stale and falling into a rut. That has been my experience. When I have concentrated for some time on a piece of creative writing or confined myself to book reviews, or read and thought about nothing but history, I have to make a change and correct my vision with other perspectives; I must turn for a while to philosophy or the history of music, or paint, or in any case do something else. Before giving ourselves a jolt and making a change, we usually go through a period of great listlessness and depression.

[576]

Man, to cite the fine old image, consists of body, soul, and mind. Most often, two of these elements form an alliance and the third is neglected. In Christianity an alliance of mind and soul slandered and neglected the body. In our times the body and mind are overcultivated at the expense of the soul. Art is eminently the realm of the soul, yet encompasses the mind and body.

[577]

All life is a becoming, not a being. Consequently, what you call "culture" is not something finished once and for all, that we can inherit and preserve or throw away and destroy. Only so much of our culture remains alive and effective as each generation is able to gain possession of and breathe life into.

[578]

In the moment when a piece of literature encounters an intelligent and independent reader, something new and living is born: the author's individuality and world of images enter into combinations and mixtures with the reader's character and associations. In readers of my own works, I have often met with interpretations which never occurred to me when I was writing and which were nevertheless quite admissible and legitimate.

[579]

In the end human judgment always prevails over aesthetic judgment. We do not easily forgive misuse of talent, but in a work of human value we are prepared to forgive obvious formal weaknesses.

[580]

"Proficiency" does not inspire love. But intense feeling, an intense inner dream, even when expressed almost awkwardly, give us confidence and awaken love. The virtuosi with their successes and sales figures are short-lived; but despite the touchingly few copies sold, Stifter's *Nachsommer* [*Indian Summer*] has forged a circle of staunch and fervent gratitude around it.

[581]

HUMOR

Humor

HUMOR IS ALWAYS somehow bourgeois, though the dyed-in-the-wool bourgeois is incapable of understanding it.

[582]

To live in the world as though it were not the world, to observe the law and yet to be above it, to possess "as though one did not possess," to renounce as though no renunciation were involved—only humor is able to live up to these revered and often formulated demands of a noble philosophy of life.

[583]

The greater a comedian is, the more gruesomely and helplessly he reduces our stupidity to the comic formula, the more we have to laugh! How people love to laugh! They flock from the suburbs in the bitter cold, they stand in line, pay money, and stay out until past midnight, only in order to laugh awhile.

[584]

Humor is a crystal that forms only amid deep and lasting sorrow. Healthy people slap their thighs and roar with laughter, but they are always perplexed and somewhat offended when from time to time they read such items as this: Inconceivable as it may seem, X, the popular and successful comedian, has drowned himself in an access of melancholia.

[585]

Humorists may write what they like, but all their titles and subjects are a mere pretext. In reality they have only one subject: the strange sadness and frustration of human life and amazement at the fact that this wretched life can nevertheless be so beautiful.

[586]

Tragedy and humor are not antitheses, or rather they are antitheses only because the one calls so relentlessly for the other.

[587]

All higher humor begins with ceasing to take oneself seriously.

[588]

HAPPINESS

Happiness

Happiness is a how, not a what; a talent, not an object.
[589]

To be able to throw oneself away for the sake of a moment, to be able to sacrifice years for a woman's smile—that is happiness.
[590]

I am sometimes inclined to think that happy people are secretly wise, even when they seem to be stupid. For what is stupider and what makes one more unhappy than intelligence?
[591]

Luck has nothing to do with reason or morality, it is magical in essence, something pertaining to an early, youthful phase of mankind. The lucky innocent, showered with gifts by the fairies, pampered by the gods, is not a fit object of rational thought, he is a symbol transcending the personal and historical. Nevertheless, it is impossible not to think of "luck" in connection with certain exceptional men, if only because they and the task appropriate to them actually managed to find each other . . . and because they were not born too early or too late.
[592]

When the ways of friends converge, the whole world looks like home for an hour.

[593]

The overvaluation of the minute, hurry as the essence of our form of life—these are undoubtedly the most dangerous enemies of joy. As much as possible as quickly as possible—that is the watchword. The consequence is more and more amusement and less and less joy.

[594]

The wonderful thing about all joy is that it comes unearned and can never be bought.

[595]

A hankering after the "happiness" of the stupid and vulgar is not necessarily a stigma of the elect. Perhaps every man, though not always with the same degree of awareness, envies the "happiness" of those who stand one step above or one step below him. Perhaps every living creature envies every other, and finds his own fate harder than all others.

[596]

When a ray of sunshine falls on a dreary street from a cloudy sky, it makes no difference what it shines on: a bottle shard on the ground, a tattered poster on the wall, or the flaxen blond of a child's head; it brings light, brings magic, transforms and transfigures.

[597]

Paradise does not make itself known as paradise until we have been driven out of it.

[598]

In the presence of the most beautiful things we always experience not only pleasure but also grief or fear.

[599]

The wanderer has the best and most delicate of all pleasures, because in addition to savoring all joys he also has the knowledge of their transience. He does not look back for long at what he has lost and does not yearn to strike roots in every place where he has been happy. There are travelers who return to the same place year after year, and there are many who cannot take leave of a beautiful sight without resolving to come back soon again. These may be good people, but good wanderers they are not. In them there is something of the lover's heavy drunkenness and something of the careful flower picker's collecting instinct. But the spirit of the wanderer—the serenity, the joyful gravity, the perpetual leave-taking—is akin to them.

[600]

Happiness can be possessed only so long as it is unseen.

[601]

The secret of my happiness was that of dream happiness: the freedom to experience everything conceivable at once, to interchange inside and outside with ease, to move space and time about like stage props.

[602]

Where we find something that resembles music, there we must stay; there is nothing else worth striving for in life than the feeling of music, the feeling of resonance and rhythmic life, or a harmony that justifies our existence.

[603]

The first requisite of happiness is freedom from time, hence from fear and hope. Most people lose this freedom as they grow older.

[604]

Think of your being as a deep lake with a small surface. The surface is consciousness. Here all is brightness, and it is here that what we call thinking takes place. But this surface is infinitely small. It may be the most beautiful, most interesting part of the lake, for in contact with the air and light the water is transformed and enriched. But the particles of water at the surface change unceasingly. They rise, they fall; there are always currents, displacements, shifts; every particle of water wants to be on the surface at some time. —Now just as the lake consists of water, so our self or soul (the word does not matter) consists of thousands and millions of particles, of an ever-increasing, ever-changing store of possessions, memories, impressions. Of all this our consciousness sees only the small surface. The soul itself does not see the infinitely larger part of its content. A soul, it seems to me, is rich and healthy and capable of happiness when there is a constant exchange, a mutual renewal, between the great darkness and the small field of light. Most people have within them thousands and thousands of things that never rise to the bright surface, that rot in the depths and torment them. Because these things rot and bring torment, they are rejected time and again by consciousness, which distrusts and fears them. This is the substance of the morality that says: What has been recognized as harmful must not be allowed to rise to the surface! But nothing is harmful and nothing useful, everything is good or everything is indifferent. Each one of us has within him things that belong to him, things that are truly his own, but are not permitted to emerge. If they did, says morality, a calamity would ensue! But quite possibly it would be a stroke of good fortune! Therefore let everything rise to the surface. The man who submits to a morality is impoverishing himself.

[605]

Beauty derives a part of its magic from its transience.

[606]

People seldom make each other happy with duty and morality and commandments, because they do not make themselves happy. It may be possible for a man to be "good," but only if he is happy.

[607]

Happiness is love, nothing else. A man who is capable of love is happy.

[608]

LOVE

Love

Nowadays it is thought to be not only possible but even normal and sensible for a gifted, vigorous, intelligent man to spend all his talents and energies on making money or on serving a political party; it would never enter anyone's head that he might expend these talents and energies on women and love. In no truly "modern view of life"—from ultra-bourgeois middle America to reddest Soviet Russia—is love looked upon as anything more than an insignificant, secondary pleasure factor, which can be regulated in accordance with the principles of hygiene.

[609]

Love is an astonishing thing, even in art. It can do what no amount of culture, criticism, or intellect can do, namely, connect the most widely divergent poles, bring together what is oldest and what is newest. It transcends time by relating everything to itself as a center. It alone gives certainty, it alone is right, because it has no interest in being right.

[610]

Imagination and empathy are nothing other than forms of love.

[611]

It is a strange but simple secret, known to the wisdom of all epochs, that every act of selfless devotion, of sympathy and love, however slight, makes us richer, whereas every striving for possessions and power robs us and makes us poorer. The Indians knew this and taught it, then the wise Greeks, and then Jesus. It has been known and taught by thousands of wise men and poets, whose works have outlived their time, whereas the rich men and kings of their day are forgotten. Your preference may lie with Jesus or Plato, with Schiller or Spinoza; in all of them you will find the ultimate wisdom, the message that neither power nor possessions nor knowledge brings happiness, but love alone. In every act of selflessness, of loving sacrifice, of compassion, every renunciation of self, we seem to be giving something away, to be robbing ourselves. The truth is that such acts enrich us and make us grow; this is the only way that leads forward and upward. It's an old song, and I am a poor singer and preacher, but truths do not grow old, they are true always and everywhere, whether preached in the desert, sung in a song, or printed in a newspaper.

[612]

It is the same with love as with art: the man who can love great things just a little is poorer than the man who can love the little things passionately.

[613]

If we can cheer someone up and make him happier, we should do so by all means.

[614]

To love and to know prove to be pretty much the same thing; as a rule the people we know best are those we love best.

[615]

Love must neither beg nor demand. Love must be strong
enough to find certainty within itself. Then it ceases to be
moved and becomes the mover.

[616]

He had loved and in loving found himself. Yet most men
love in order to lose themselves.

[617]

Without self-love it is impossible to love our fellow men.
Self-hatred is exactly the same thing as blatant egoism; it
leads in the end to the same cruel isolation and despair.

[618]

There is nothing a man can love so much as himself.
There is nothing a man can fear as much as himself.
Consequently, along with the other mythologies, com-
mandments, and religions of primitive man, there arose
that strange system of transference and delusion in which
self-love, the very foundation of life, was forbidden, hence
condemned to be concealed and masked. To love another
was held to be better, more ethical, and nobler than to
love oneself. But then, since self-love was the primary
drive and love of others was never really able to compete
with it, men invented a masked, sublimated, stylized self-
love, consisting of mutual love among members of a
group. That is how the family, the clan, the village, the
religious community, the people, the nation became
sacrosanct.

[619]

The commandment to love, whether taught by Jesus or by
Goethe, has been utterly misunderstood by the world. It
was not a commandment at all. There are no command-

ments. Commandments are misinterpreted truths. The root of all wisdom is: Happiness springs only from love. But to say, "Love thy neighbor as thyself!" is already a falsification. It would be much better to say, "Love thyself as thy neighbor"! Perhaps the original error was beginning with the neighbor.

[620]

To be loved is not happiness. Every man loves himself. To love: that is happiness.

[621]

For two human beings who are dependent on one another to live at peace is the rarest and most difficult of ethical and intellectual accomplishments.

[622]

What would reason and sobriety be without knowledge of intoxication; what would sensual pleasure be if death were not behind it; and what would love be without the eternal deadly enmity of the sexes?

[623]

I learned above all that these baubles, the articles of fashion and luxury, are not mere trumpery and kitsch, the invention of grasping manufacturers and dealers, but justified, beautiful, and varied, a small or, rather, a large world of objects, all of which—from powder and perfume to dancing slippers, from rings to cigarette cases, from belt buckles to handbags—have only one purpose: to serve love, to refine the senses, to breathe life into a dead environment, and to endow us by magic with new organs of love. This handbag was no handbag, this purse was no purse, these flowers no flowers, this fan no fan, all were the palpable substance of love, of magic, of courtship; they were messengers, smugglers, weapons, battle cries.

[624]

Most of what we do in life, even if we advance other reasons, is done because of women.

[625]

I am a devotee of infidelity, of change, of imagination. I see no reason for fastening my love to any particular spot on this earth. I believe that what we love is never anything more than a symbol. When our love becomes fixed, when it turns to fidelity and virtue, it arouses my suspicions.

[626]

Everything in the world can be imitated and forged, everything but love. Love can be neither stolen nor imitated; it lives only in hearts that are able to give themselves wholly. It is the source of all art.

[627]

People are reluctant to pay with confidence and love; they prefer to pay with money and goods.

[628]

Everyone knows from experience how easy it is to fall in love and how difficult and beautiful it is to love truly. Like all true values, love cannot be bought. Pleasure can be bought, but not love.

[629]

Nothing is more futile than thinking about someone we love. Such thoughts are like certain folk songs, in which thousands of things turn up but the refrain keeps recurring, even where it doesn't fit.

[630]

Love alone gives life meaning. That is: the more capable we are of loving and surrendering ourselves, the more meaningful our life becomes.

[631]

It may be the business of great thinkers to unmask the world and despise it. But to me only one thing is important: the ability to love the world, to contemplate it and myself and all other beings with love and wonder and veneration.

[632]

What you call "will" is a kind of ethic or morality, fed by unconscious instinctual forces. I do not think it is necessarily desirable that we ourselves should be able to decide when to be happy and when to be sad and to justify our choice by reason. From the standpoint of reason and logic, life offers occasion neither for joy nor for sorrow. But we can utterly destroy the value, the life, and the meaning of our "moods" by subjecting them to too much reason. This can best be seen by the example of love. Who ever loved because of reason or will? No, love is something that happens to us, but the more we give ourselves to it, the stronger it makes us.

[633]

We overestimate everything we pin our love on, and for this reason it sometimes requires contradiction and criticism, for love alone is living and precious, not the object we pin it on.

[634]

DEATH

Death

DEATH AGONY, no less than childbirth, is a life process, and often one can mistake the one for the other.

[635]

After every death, life becomes more delicate and precious.

[636]

The call of death is also a call of love. Death becomes sweet when we say yes to it, when we accept it as one of the great and eternal forms of life and transformation.

[637]

The rational man believes that the earth was given to man for his use. His most dreaded enemy is death, the thought that his life and activity are transient. He avoids thinking of death, and when the thought pursues him, he takes refuge in activity, he fights off death with redoubled striving: for possessions, for knowledge, for laws, for rational mastery of the world. His immortality is his belief in progress: he believes that as an active link in the endless chain of progress he will never entirely cease to be.

[638]

We should never repent of steps we have taken or of deaths we have died.

[639]

It seems to me that when a man's nature, education, and circumstances forbid him to commit suicide, he will be unable to do so, even if his imagination sometimes tempts him with this solution. When this is not the case and a man resolutely casts away a life that has become unbearable to him, he is, I believe, as much entitled to his suicide as others to a natural death. I have felt the death of some men who have made away with themselves to be more natural and meaningful than that of a good many who died a natural death.

[640]

A man dies so damned slowly, bit by bit: every tooth, muscle, and bone takes leave individually, as though we had been especially intimate with it.

[641]

Grief and lamentation are our first natural response to the loss of someone we loved. They help us through our first anguish; but they do not suffice to forge a bond between us and the dead.

On the primitive level, this is accomplished by the cult of the dead: sacrifices, decoration of the tomb, monuments, flowers. But at our level the sacrifice to the dead must take place in our own souls, through thoughts, through exacting memory, whereby we reconstruct the loved one within us. If we can do this, the dead live on by our side, their image is saved and helps to make our grief fruitful.

[642]

Death

I need no weapon against death, because there is no death. What does exist is the fear of death. That can be cured.

[643]

In the essentials of what they meant to us, the dead live on with us as long as we ourselves live. Sometimes we can speak to them and take counsel of them more readily than with the living.

[644]

YOUTH AND OLD AGE

Youth and Old Age

I BELIEVE that a very definite dividing line can be drawn between youth and old age. Youth ceases with egoism, old age begins when we begin to live for others.
[645]

Emphasis on youth and the organization of the young have never been to my liking; basically, only the commonplace are young or old; all more gifted, more highly differentiated beings are sometimes old, sometimes young, just as they are sometimes gay and sometimes sad.
[646]

An adult who has learned to transform a part of his feelings into thoughts misses these thoughts in a child and imagines that the feelings themselves are absent.
[647]

On the road from youth to manhood there are two principal steps: to become aware of one's own ego and to integrate this ego with the community. The simpler and less problematic a young man is, the less difficulty he will have with these tasks. More talented and highly differentiated men have a harder time of it, most of all those to whom some specific talent does not show the way. But every life is a venture and in every instance a balance must be arrived at between a man's personal gifts and drives and the demands of society. This is never done without sacrifices and mistakes. Even we old people who seem to have achieved success and stability are not above doubts and mistakes; we live in the very thick of them.

[648]

Anyone who cannot abide one-sidedness and a daring spirit of revolt, anyone who would rather see young people wise, kindly, and all-understanding than fanatical and puritanical, had better keep away from them. He himself will be the loser.

[649]

The revolt against big names and ready-made historical constructions is something youthful. It is not good or bad, it is a right and instinct of the young (who need not be identified according to calendar years).

[650]

I understand the youthful, idealistic contempt for money. Yet in the present form of our society, money is not only a blind and evil power, but something else as well: it is the concentrated yield of work, privation, saving, and recti-tude. Consequently every father who has saved slowly, little by little, is sensitive about the gestures with which his children show their contempt for money.

[651]

An old family's loving attachment to its house and home is a fine thing, but the only way in which a family can achieve new youth and greatness is for the sons to aim at higher goals than those of their fathers.

[652]

The revolutionary outcry of certain young people should not be taken too seriously. The only serious part of it is a profound need to find new emotional outlets and new expressions for their new concerns.

[653]

The younger generation feel that the whole decades-old bourgeois world, under whose petty tyranny they grew up, is disintegrating. They are overjoyed, and rightly so.

[654]

Just as "knowledge," that is, the awakening of consciousness, is represented in the Bible as a sin (symbolized by the serpent in the Garden of Eden), so the process of growing to manhood, individuation, the struggle of the individual to single himself out from the mass and achieve personality, is always regarded by morality and tradition with distrust. Friction between youth and family, between father and son, is something natural and as old as the hills, yet to every father it is outrageous and unprecedented rebellion.

[655]

Truth is a typical ideal of the young, and love an ideal of the mature. Thinking men lose their enthusiasm for the truth when they discover that man is singularly ill-equipped for determining the objective truth, and that consequently the quest for truth cannot be the human, humane activity par excellence. But even those who never arrive at such insights undergo the same change in the course of their unconscious experience. To possess the truth, to be right, to be able to distinguish good and evil with certainty, consequently to be able and under obligation to judge, punish, condemn, and wage war—that is youthful and befits the young. When a man grows older and clings to these ideals, his capacity—none too strong to begin with—to "awaken," to sense the superhuman truth inherent in us humans, withers away.

[656]

Older people can be expected to deal in a freer, more kindly, more playful and sophisticated way with their own capacity for love than is possible for the young. Old people always tend to find the young precocious. Yet old people often imitate the gestures and ways of the young; they themselves are fanatical, unjust, self-righteous, and easily offended. Age is not worse than youth, Lao-tse is not worse than Buddha, blue is not worse than red. Age is inferior only when it tries to impersonate youth.

[657]

Aging as such is a natural process. A man of sixty-five or seventy-five is just as healthy as one of thirty or fifty, as long as he does not try to be younger than he is. Unfortunately, people do not always keep pace with their age; inwardly, they often race ahead of it, and still more often they lag behind it—then consciousness and life-feeling are less mature than the body, resist its natural development, and make demands on themselves that they are unable to meet.

[658]

Only in growing older do we see how rare beauty is and how miraculous it is that flowers can bloom in the midst of factories and cannon, that poetry can survive in the midst of newspapers and stock reports.

[659]

A young man's most essential need is to be able to take himself seriously. The mature man's need is to be able to sacrifice himself, because there is something higher than himself that he takes seriously. The life of the spirit must move between these two poles. For the task and yearning of youth is to become, whereas the mature man's task is to give himself away or, as the German mystics said it, to "unbecome." Before a man can sacrifice his personality, he must become a complete man, a personality, and suffer the torments of this individuation.

[660]

SOURCES

Sources

WORKS AVAILABLE IN ENGLISH TRANSLATION

UNTRANSLATED WORKS

Sources

361, 369, 377, 387, 389, 390, 391, 393, 394, 406, 408, 429, 439,
461, 462, 470, 482, 485, 516, 523, 525, 526, 528, 542, 543, 548,
554, 566, 581, 598, 627

Schriften zur Literatur, I (Writings on Literature, Volume One)
25, 36, 96, 142, 153, 164, 167, 252, 265, 273, 348, 370, 371,
372, 374, 378, 379, 381, 385, 388, 398, 448, 476, 480, 495, 508,
517, 520, 521, 527, 530, 531, 532, 537, 541, 546, 549, 555,
580, 610, 613, 615, 649, 650, 654, 657

Schriften zur Literatur, II (Writings on Literature, Volume Two)
131, 155, 183, 197, 268, 276, 293, 294, 341, 386, 426, 468, 488,
497, 500, 534, 538, 539, 565, 567, 597, 609

Späte Prosa (Late Prose) 160, 230, 604

Tagebuch 1920/21 (Diary 1920/21) 161, 223, 238, 286, 287,
484, 551

Traumfährte (Dream Journeys) 200, 236, 259, 260, 312, 333,
444, 552, 591